A Short History of Korea

A SHORT HISTORY
OF KOREA

Compiled by

THE CENTRE FOR EAST ASIAN
CULTURAL STUDIES

THE CENTRE FOR EAST ASIAN CULTURAL STUDIES
TOKYO
EAST WEST CENTER PRESS
HONOLULU

c/o The Toyo Bunko
147, Kamifujimae-cho, Bunkyo-ku, Tokyo

This book was originally published with
the assistance of UNESCO, in implementation of
the Major Project on
Mutual Appreciation of Eastern and Western Cultural Values.

Distributed outside Japan by
EAST WEST CENTER PRESS
HONOLULU, HAWAII 96822

Printed in Japan by
KASAI PUBLISHING & PRINTING CO.
(*Pan-Pacific Press*)
Minato-ku, Tokyo.

2nd printing, July, 1964

NOTE

This volume is based on the 172-page booklet by an anonymous author, *Chōsen-shi no Shirube* (Korean History Handbook), which was published by the Government-General of Chōsen in 1937. In this English version, however, some passages in the original that were heavily Japan-centered have been omitted and corrections have been made, including an entirely new chapter on the period of Japanese rule of Korea up to 1945.

CONTENTS

Maps

1

PERIODS

Before discussing the history of Korea in this small book, it would be well to give first a rough description of the periodization most frequently used by historians. According to the customary system, the entire course of this peninsula country's history is divided into the following six periods:
1) Ancient Ch'ao-hsien Kingdoms
2) Lo-lang Province and the Three Hans
3) Three Kingdoms
4) Unified Silla
5) Koryŏ
6) Chosŏn (Yi Dynasty)
The period of Ancient Ch'ao-hsien Kingdoms actually covers two eras. The first is the reign of Chi-tzŭ (Ki-ja), a prince of the Yin Dynasty of China and his descendants, corresponding to the Chou and Ch'in Dynasties in Chinese history. The second is the dynasty founded by Wei Man (Wiman) who was exiled from Yen State in Northern China in the Former Han period and replaced a descendant of Chi-tzŭ.

The period of the Lo-lang Province and the Three Hans, which followed the Ancient Ch'ao-hsien Kingdoms, goes back some 2,000 years. To be exact, it was in 108 B.C. that Wu-ti, the famous Emperor of Han, defeated Wei You-ch'ü, a grandson of Wei Man, captured the Korean Peninsula and governed it by dividing it into four provinces. Lo-lang was one of these provinces, the other three being Lin-t'un, Hsüan-t'u and Chen-fan. Lin-t'un and Chen-fan were abolished in 25 years followed by Hsüan-t'u, and before long Lo-lang with its political center in the present P'yŏngyang became the only province in all of Korea. Thus the period came to be known by that name.

The Lo-lang Province ceased to exist in 313 A.D. after lasting some 400 years. The last 100 years of the period are sometimes known as the Lo-lang-Tai-fang period, because another province, Tai-fang, was in existence in the southern part of Lo-lang during that time.

However, about the same time as the Lo-lang era, a people known as Han occupied the southern part of the Korean Peninsula. They were composed of three sub-groups: Ma-han, Che'n-han and Pien-ch'en. They were usually known as San-han (Three Hans). Thus this 400-year period is generally called the Lo-lang-San-han period.

Lo-lang Province was overthrown by the Koguryŏ people who moved southward from the upper reaches of the Yalu River. Together with Paekche and Silla, two nations which grew out of the Three Hans, Koguryŏ composed the Three Kingdoms. The era of the Three Kingdoms lasted for about 350 years after the Lo-lang Province perished. It ended when Paekche and Koguryŏ were conquered by the T'ang (China) to leave only Silla as an independent nation on the Korean Peninsula.

The transition of rulers went on rather uneventfully thereafter. The 260-year Silla period was succeeded by the Koryŏ period of the Wang Family which lasted 460 years. Finally, there came the Chosŏn Dynasty of the Yi Family which ruled Korea for half a millennium.

2

DAWN OF THE KOREAN
PENINSULA

The days of the Ancient Ch'ao-hsien Kingdoms saw the dawn of culture on the Korean Peninsula. The first state on the peninsula to appear in historical documents, however faintly, is the Ch'ao-hsien Principate of Chi-tzŭ who was a prince of the late Yin Dynasty of China. This Principate, also called Chi Dynasty, lasted until about 200 B.C.

The second state to appear on the peninsula was the Ch'ao-hsien Kingdom established by Wei Man who overthrew the Chi Dynasty. Like Chi-tzŭ, Wei Man, a former subject of Yen, was an exile from China.

Chi Chun, the ruler of Ch'ao-hsien at that time, trusted the Chinese exile and awarded him a post of great importance only to be betrayed and driven off the throne. Wei Man became the ruler but his descendants ruled for only three generations—less than 100 years—before their kingdom was conquered by Wu-ti, the great Emperor of Han China.

The political and cultural center in the days of the Ancient Kingdoms is believed to have been situated in the area where P'yŏngyang now stands—also the seat of the Lo-lang Provincial Government. Thus the basin along the Taedong River is considered the setting of the origin of Korean culture.

Among the tribes which lived in the neighboring areas and received the benefits of this culture through contact with the two Kingdoms of Ancient Korea, were Chen-fan and Lint'un; if the scope of influence is interpreted more widely, such tribes as Wei and Mo might also be included. Worthy of note during this period is the submission of Nan-lü, the chief of Wei in the east, with his 280,000 subjects, to Han about 20 years before the fall of the Wei Dynasty (about 128 B.C.). The Chinese established a new province named Ts'ang-hai in the area where Nan-lü's people lived. Although the exact location of this province is not known, and the province existed for only three years, there is little doubt that Nan-lü was a tribal chief in Korea. The fact that a Chinese province was established in that area prior to the founding of the four provinces, such as Lo-lang is significant, as it indicates a direct extension of political rule by Han China. A more detailed explanation of this period is needed before we proceed to the Lo-lang era.

From archaeological chronology, the establishment of a Chinese province among the native Korean tribes means the importation of metal ware into the stone age.

Leaving the historical documents for a moment, let us consider the relics and remains left by the inhabitants of the Korean Peninsula in those ancient days and spread roughly all over the peninsula. Those which are archaeologically considered the most ancient are similar to those discovered in Japan and Manchuria. It is only natural that concentrations of remains are found along the shores of the Yellow Sea and the Japan Sea on the east and west sides of the peninsula, and along such rivers as the Yalu, the Tumen, the Taedong, the Han and the Naktong. But in Korea and Manchuria vestiges of these ancient people are also found, not only in places near rivers and seashores, but in hills and on mountain tops. This phenomenon is a continental peculiarity.

From remains unearthed, it is apparent that the inhabitants of the peninsula had contact with the Chinese who moved down from North China. Ming-tao and An-yang-pu coins circulated in the Ch'an-Kuo Period of China and metal including bronze swords and iron halberds of the Ch'in and Han period of China have been found throughout the peninsula at such places as Yongyŏn-dong, Sungjŏng-myŏn,

Uiwŏn-gun; Taeyu-dong, Tongch'ang-myŏn, Ch'angsŏng-gun; and Togwan-dong, Namsinhyŏn-myŏn, Nyongbyŏn-gun, of P'yŏngan-pukto; Onyang-ni, Onhwa-myŏn, Nyŏngwŏn-gun of P'yŏngan-namdo; Muan-gun and Sand-hang, Cheju-do, of Ch'ŏlla-namdo; and Hoehyŏn-ni, Kimhae-myŏn, Kimhae-gun, of K'yŏngsang-namdo.

Shown on the map, these places indicate the route along which the Chinese moved southward and the ancient China-Korea traffic. This leads to the assumption that the southern part of the peninsula and the coastal areas were the first to have any contact with Chinese culture.

The introduction of metal ware into a stone age community inevitably results in the birth of a new culture, that is, a metal-stone age where the two types of community overlap each other. Remains show that the present P'yŏngan-namdo, P'yŏngan-pukto and Hwanghae-do were the first to enter this new era on the peninsula. This coincides roughly with the assumption based on documents that the areas along the Taedong River were the center of the Ancient Ch'ao-hsien Kingdoms. The tendency towards a concentration of cultural activity in these areas became even clearer with the establishment of the Lo-lang and other provinces.

3

RISE AND FALL OF THE LO-LANG

As mentioned in the previous chapter, Emperor Wu-ti of Han set up the Ts'ang-hai Province about 20 years before establishing the four provinces on the Korean Peninsula. However, the Ts'ang-hai Province perished after only three years' existence. In 109 B.C. Emperor Wu-ti sent his forces both by land and sea to capture Wang-chien-chêng, the capital of Wei Man's Korea or the present P'yŏngyang. The capital fell in the following summer and the Emperor set up the four provinces of Lo-lang, Chen-fan, Lin-t'un and Hsüan-t'u. Of these, Lin-t'un and Hsüan-t'u were named after the native tribes occupying the area.

Generally, it is believed that Lo-lang covered an area extending approximately from P'yŏngan-do and Hwanghae-do to Kyŏnggi-do with its center situated along the Taedong River; Chen-fan occupied Ch'ungch'ŏng-do and Chŏlla-do, Lin-t'un covered Kangwŏn-do and Hsüan-t'u, Hamgyŏng-do. There is an opposing theory, however, about the location of Chen-fan Province, which places it to the north of Lo-lang, along the upper streams of the Yalu River and the southwest foothills of the Long White Mountains.

But these provinces were drastically reduced in size only 26 years after being formed. Chen-fan and Lin-t'un were totally abolished and most of Hsüan-t'u was abandoned. Part of what was left of Hsüan-t'u was annexed to Lo-lang and the rest were governed from the provincial capital, which was moved to the north side of the Yalu River.

Thus Lo-lang was left as the only province on the Korean Peninsula ruled by the Chinese until Tai-fang Province was created in about 204 A.D. by separating a southern part of Lo-lang. These two provinces lasted until near the end of the Western Chin Dynasty of China some 100 years later, putting an end to the era of provinces established by the Chinese. The following is a brief synopsis of the history of the Chinese colony:

Provinces of Lo-lang, Chen-fan,
    Lin-t'un, Hsüan-t'u   108 B.C. – 82 B.C.
Province of Lo-lang   82 B.C. – c. 204 A.D.
Provinces of Lo-lang, Tai-fang   c. 204 A.D. – 313 A.D.

Remains unearthed from ancient tombs outside P'yŏng-yang City indicate that the tools and products of life at that

time were rather advanced. Politically speaking, however, it
was a rather unstable period as reflected in the shift of population among the provinces recorded in Chinese documents.
It is shown in the following, covering a period from about
110 years after the establishment of the four provinces to
about 140 years later, toward the end of the two provinces:

Chap. on Geography,		households	persons	counties
Ch'ien-Han-shu	Lo-lang	62,812	406,748	25
Chap. on Geography,				
Hou-Han-shu	Lo-lang	61,492	257,050	18
Chap. on Geography,				
Chin-shu	Lo-lang	3,700		6
	Tai-fang	4,900		7

The residents of these provinces governed by the Chinese
officials were composed of the descendants of Chinese im-
migrants and native Koreans, the latter greatly outnumber-
ing the former. The gradual reduction of countries and
provinces was mainly due to resistance from the dissident
natives. The abandonment and final downfall of the provinces is ilkely to have been caused as much by the rise of the
oppressed natives as by the decline of the Chinese on the
mainland.

The entire Lo-lang era, which moved on a gradual down-
ward course after reaching its highest point immediately
after being established, witnessed a continual struggle between the Chinese and the Koreans. The setting up of Tai-
fang Province was an attempt to restore the Chinese reign
in Lo-lang by cutting away an area where dissident Koreans
were most rampant.

Tai-fang was originally the name of a country in the
province of Lo-lang. Toward the end of the Han Dynasty,
several cities in the southern part of Lo-lang were occupied
by native tribes of Han and Wei. After the Kung-sun family,
which rose to power in the Liao-tung area, put Lo-lang under

control, they separated the southern part, made it an independent province and gave it the name of the country in the area.

After this renewal of Chinese reign, the natives in the southern part of the peninsula reestablished their relations with Tai-fang. The new province also opened the way for active contact with the western part of Japan. Later, however, Tai-fang was captured by tribes of the Han in the south, while Koguryŏ tribesmen in the north seized Lo-lang.

4

HAN AND WEI PEOPLES

The southern part of the Korean Peninsula, south of Lo-lang Province, has found its way into very ancient documents as the "Land of Han", meaning probably the place where the Hans or the Han tribe lived. Legend has it that when Wei Man captured Ch'ao-hsien, which was ruled by the descendants of Chi-tzŭ, the dethroned king escaped into the Land of Han with his vassals and assumed the title of the King of Han. It is also said that in the days of Wei Man's rule some of his key retainers migrated to Han.

In the early part of the third century when Tai-fang Province was established, the Han tribe was divided into Ma-han, Ch'en-han and Pien-ch'en. Ma-han was composed of 56 small states, and Ch'en-han and Pien-ch'en each had 12. It is believed that each of these states had its own chief. Ch'en-han was ruled by a sovereign called the King of Ch'en although how great his power was and how influential he was are unknown. It can be said that each group was not solidly unified. Interestingly, the chief of each state had a

Iron Implements,
Northern Korea

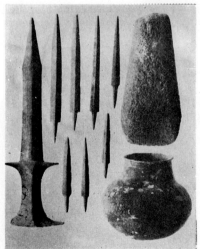

Stone Implements and
a Pottery,
Southern Korea

Brick-chamber, a Tomb of
Lo-lang

Lacquer Basket
(Part), Lo-lang

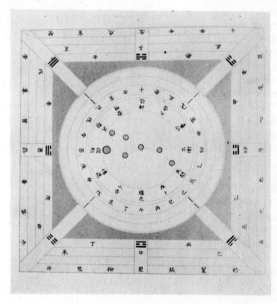

Divination Diagram (Reconstruction), Lo-lang

Chinese name of office. The Chinese title was given to them
in return for their visits to the Province regularly and pay-
ment of annual taxes and offering of labor whenever necessary. It can be safely assumed that agricultural and marine
products constituted most of the taxes, although iron presented from Ch'ien-han is also well known.

While the Hans occupied the southern part of the peninsula, the Wei tribe lived in the district where the Lin-t'un
Province, now known as Kangwŏn-do, was located and the
Wo-chü tribe shared the area assigned as the Hsüan-t'u
Province, or Hamgyŏng-do of today. These two tribes had
relations with neighboring Chinese provinces similar to those
the Han had. The Wo-chü commanded strong influence in
their area—strong enough to drive the Hsüan-t'u Province
across the Yalu River in the end—and retained the ancient
Chinese system in their political organization. These facts
show that for some four centuries beginning in 100 B.C.,
Chinese culture under the dynasties of Han, Wei and Chin
was transplanted in the Korean Peninsula, at least in the
areas where Chinese provinces existed.

This new culture introduced by the Chinese was so highly
advanced and removed from the indigeneous culture, that we
assume today that the native Koreans were unable to as-
similate it and develop their own culture. Thus, essentially,
the transplanted culture was destined to have a short life,
dying with the provinces and cities established by the
Chinese.

However, the Chinese culture which flourished on the Korean Peninsula for four centuries did not disappear completely, without leaving some trace of its influence on the
Korean culture. In fact, many legacies of Chinese culture
are found in various phases of Korean life. One of the
major influences was the introduction of metal ware. Another
was the adoption of the system of political control which
was introduced to the Koreans whose political and social

systems were still undeveloped.

The chiefs of local communities had roles as officials of the provinces or cities in the newly enforced political organization. It is believed that the chiefs of the Han and Wei tribes developed their power rapidly taking advantage of this new political system, and in further natural development after the collapse of the Chinese-ruled provinces and cities, these local chiefs assumed power and governed their communities. Silla and Paekche were the two powers to survive the power struggles to unify various local areas under Mahan and Ch'en-han.

The Chinese influence was also apparent in the fields of religion and philosophy. In this connection, a divination dial unearthed from ancient tombs of the Lo-lang age has drawn the attention of scholars. The device is made of a square board representing the earth and a round plate symbolizing the sky. The sky disk bore the Great Bear, names of the gods of 12 months, the 10 celestial stems and 12 terrestrial branches, while the earth square carried the eight signs of divination, 12 terrestrial branches and the 28 solar-stages along the zodiac. By adjusting the two boards, soothsayers told fortunes. The theory concerning the positive and the negative principles of Chinese philosophy with its five natural elements and agriculture themes must have been among the earliest philosophies to be brought to the Koreans by the Chinese.

Next to be considered are the relations of the two provinces of Tai-fang and Lo-lang with Japan across the sea via Han. Japanese myths and legends indicate that the occupants of the Japanese Islands crossed to the Korean Peninsula from very ancient times. This is substantiated by old Chinese documents concerning Lo-lang Province. These records show that the Japanese not only visited Korea but also reached the Chinese mainland in the very early period of history.

According to Chinese chronicles, envoys from Japan (then

known as *Wo*) visited China as early as 57 A.D. After Lo-lang Province was set up, the China-Japan trade was carried out through this province on the Peninsula until it was suspended in 266 A.D. It is considered today that the discontinuation of relations is attributable to the prevailing political situation in the southern part of the peninsula.

Old Chinese sources show that Japan's influence was strongest in Pien-ch'en, which is believed to have been situated in an area near the mouth of the Naktong River. Pien-ch'en is the state mentioned as *Mimana* in ancient Japanese history; the origin of *Mimana* can be traced back to the days of Lo-lang Province. A notable change in the political position in the Korean Peninsula of Pien-ch'en as well as two other Hans, which served as relay stations for Japanese trade with the Chinese, can be found in old documents. That is, from 261 A.D. to 290 A.D., emissaries from Ma-han and Ch'en-han, who until then paid calls only on the governments in the provinces of Lo-lang and Tai-fang, visited the Chinese capital as often as ten times. This shows the decline of the two provinces and the rise of the two Hans.

The rise of the three Hans adversely affected Japanese influence in Pien-ch'en and interrupted the Japan-China trade. Instead, the three Hans established ties with China and paid land-taxes, but relations were disrupted in 290 A.D. More than two decades later, in 313 A.D., Lo-lang Province was destroyed by Koguryŏ in the north and Tai-fang Province came under the control of the Hans. For the next 80 years, the history of the southern part of the Korean Peninsula is left blank except for the movement of Koguryŏ.

5

RISE OF KOGURYO (KAO-CHU-LI)

Koguryŏ (Kao-chü-li) had a history of 300 years before it overthrew Lo-lang Province and laid the ground for its power expansion on the peninsula. According to the legend of Koguryŏ, the tribe originated from the Fu-yü tribe in northern Manchuria and had occupied an area at the foot of the Long White Mountains by the time it made its first appearance in history around 100 B.C. Its members probably moved south along the Sungari River from their original community.

After the Hsüan-t'u Province moved in about 75 B.C. from the present Hamgyŏng-do to the north of the Yalu River, the Koguryŏ tribes led their life independently outside its boundaries. In the early days of the Latter Han Dynasty, their chief was given the title of the King of Koguryŏ, and they were usually obedient to China, receiving Han ranks and official uniforms. Yet at times they made inroads to the Province, the Koguryŏ tribesmen were put under the control of the Province but attacking also Liao-tung Province, moving across the Liao River and staging battles with the Chinese forces.

At the end of Latter Han period of China, the Kung-sun family who established the Tai-fang Province sent forces to fight Koguryŏ and finally defeated the tribe at its stronghold along the T'ung-chia River. Driven out of their city, the Koguryŏ moved south to build a new city called Wan-tu on the so-called T'ung-kou plain lying between the Yalu River and one of its tributaries, the T'ung-kou River, around 210 A.D. The City of Wan-tu, also known as the Castle of Kungnae, is believed to have been located near either the present T'ung-kou County across the river from Manp'o-jin in the P'yŏngan-pukto, or the Shan-chêng-tzu Fortress situated north of T'ung-kou. A score of ancient mounds are to be found in the area today, and a number of mounds containing a beautiful wall painting have been discovered.

The Koguryŏs, who suffered a blow at the hand of the Kung-sun family, recovered from the damage in their new stronghold and renewed their attack on Hsüan-t'u Province. When Wei Kingdom in North China attacked Wu Kingdom in the south, Koguryŏ made an alliance with Wei forcing the Kung-suns to fight on two fronts; at the same time, Koguryŏ established ties with Wu sending emissaries via the sea to the court Sun Ch'üan, on a policy of befriending distant states and antagonizing neighbors. But after the Kung-suns were destroyed by Wei in 238 A.D., Koguryŏ faced invasion from Wei and Wu. In 244 A.D., General Wu-Ch'iu Chien of Wei captured Wan-tu and, in the following year, sent the governor of Hsüan-t'u Province to drive the king of Koguryŏ far out into the land of Wo-chü or the present Hamgyŏng-do and had the governors of the Lo-lang and Tai-fang Provinces clear the eastern coast of the peninsula which had been under the control of Koguryŏ.

Koguryŏ appeared completely subdued for some time as a result of these extensive maneuvers; but the tribe again came to life and staged an offensive in the Liao-tung area during the Western Chin Period (265–316 A.D.). At this time, the provinces of Lo-lang and Tai-fang were under the control of Chang T'ung who came from Liao-tung. Chang T'ung opposed the newly risen Koguryŏ for some time but finally retreated to Liao-hsi in 313 A.D. with his subjects, to leave Lo-lang and Tai-fang entirely in the hands of Koguryŏ. Usually, this year is regarded as the last of the Lo-lang Province—just 420 years after Wu-ti of Han set up the four provinces on the peninsula.

Koguryŏ's ultimate victory is attributed to a number of

factors and causes, but the most important reasons was apparently the close unity of the tribal members and its tightly-knit organization. The tribe had five classes of peers: *Chüan-nu-pu, Chüeh-nu-pu, Shun-nu-pu, Kuan-nu-pu* and *Kuei-lou-pu.* The organization changed and grew as the tribe developed and times changed. The movement of its center to Wan-tu, which was mentioned earlier, is believed to have been one of the instances which provided an important momentum toward reshaping the organization of the tribe to meet a new situation. The building of the City of Wan-tu was an unavoidable outcome of Koguryŏ's defeat by the Kung-suns, but it gave the tribe an unexpected opportunity to recognize itself and opened the way for a new class to come to power and lay the foundation for future development and prosperity. It was about 100 years after they moved to Wan-tu that the Koguryŏ completed overthrowing the Chinese rule of Lo-lang.

For several decades after the capture of Lo-lang Province, Koguryŏ was unable to strengthen its hold on the Korean Peninsula as it was absorbed in waging war in the Liao-tung district. North China had entered into the turbulent days of the so-called Sixteen Kingdoms and Koguryŏ was absorbed with continual conflicts. Especially for a period of three years beginning in 339 A.D., the invasion of the Mu-jung family from the north dealt a damaging blow comparable to that dealt to General Wu-ch'iu Chien of Wei about a century before. The city fell to the invaders, and the tomb of the father of the King was opened and sacked. At the same time, it must be noted that there were many exiles from China into Koguryŏ in this tumultuous age and these exiled Chinese made great contribution to the development of Koguryŏ's politics and culture.

6

PAEKCHE, SILLA AND KARA

Let us now examine the situation in the south while Koguryŏ was kept busy dealing with the threat from the north.

As mentioned earlier, this was a blank period of history
and not much can be said definitely about the south. However, it is assumed that Ma-han and Ch'en-han which had
established contacts with China toward the end of the period
of Lo-lang, were finally released from Chinese control
through the destruction of Lo-lang and Tai-fang and finally
developed into the two new states of Paekche and Silla.
These two states appear in Chinese history almost simul-
taneously around 372 A.D. Although the legends of these two
states relate that their beginning was in the late first century
B.C., circumstances show that they were formed in the mid-
fourth century A.D. when Paekche was under the reign of
King Kŭnch'ogo and Silla was ruled by King Naemul.

Among the factors which worked on the emergence and
development of these two kingdoms, one of the most significant was their relations to Japan. Activities of the Japanese
people had ceased to be recorded by Chinese historians since
266 A.D. It was not until 413 A.D. that the Japanese resumed
sending envoys to the Chinese court, and after that date the
situation in Japan became more or less known to outsiders.
It is improbable that the Japanese had completely withdrawn
from the Korean Peninsula during these one and half a centuries, in view of the fact that, at the time when Paekche and
Silla were growing out of Ma-han and Ch'en-han respectively, Pien-ch'en remained disunited as Kara States or in
Japanese *Mimana*, being under the direct control of Japan
while Paekche and Silla were relatively independent, only
tied by a pledge of allegiance to Japan.

This seems to indicate that, although in the third century the Japanese influence in the Korean Peninsula had dwindled temporarily in the face of the rising Han kingdoms, the Japanese tried successfully to reestablish themselves in the Pien-ch'en area by sending a large army across the sea soon after the downfall of the two Chinese provinces in the peninsula, thus creating the *Mimana* territory to counter the strong movement of the Han kingdoms toward a unity and to prevent the realization of a unified South Korea, and resulting in a competition between Silla in the east and Paekche in west. It is true that the tripartite division of the peninsula by Silla, Paekche and the Kara group was to some extent an achievement by the Han kingdoms who had been striving toward a unified Korea.

Yet the situation cannot be regarded as a completely smooth and unhindered development, for a similar division of the peninsula had already existed in the third century, and this seems to be too slow a progress to be achieved in the course of more than one and a half centuries. Such Japanese expansion into Korea in protohistoric times has probably formed a factual core of the legend of the famed expedition to Korea by the Empress Jingū related in old Japanese chronicles in a vague, mythical way.

Moreover, there is no doubt about a deep Japanese influence on the growth of Silla and Paekche. A good corroboration to this view is found in the fact that, when Koguryŏ turned from the Liao-tung area to start a southward advance in the Korean Peninsula, she ran into stiff opposition from the Japanese sphere of influence which covered both Silla and Paekche, and that a period of Koguryŏ-Japanese rivalry over the hegemony in the peninsula had to ensue for quite some time. Usually the Three Kingdoms Period is regarded as having begun in the mid-fourth century when Silla and Paekche emerged, but in actuality it began only after the competition between Koguryŏ and Japan had subsided.

Monument
of King
Kwanggae˙to,
Koguryŏ

Mural Painting, Tomb of the Dancers, Koguryŏ

Maitreya, Bronze, Three Kingdoms

Tile with Phoenix,
Packche

Tile with Monster
Mask, Paekche

7

CONFLICT BETWEEN KOGURYO
AND JAPAN

The era of Koguryŏ-Japan conflicts is monumentalized by the Monument of King Kwanggaet'o, which looms up outside the T'ung-kou County along the Yalu River, where an ancient capital of Koguryŏ was located. The Monument was built in 414 A.D., two years after the death of the King.

The existence of the monument has been known to the Korean people for five centuries. But it was only about 80 years ago that the epitaph on the monument was deciphered and studied by Japanese and Chinese scholars. The decoding of the epitaph gave important clues to the study of the Korean Peninsula's ancient history.

The epitaph, describing the life history of King Kwanggaet'o, dealt largely with the king's "down to the South" expansion policy, and therefore touched on the struggle between Koguryŏ and Japan. The king acceded to the throne at the age of eighteen in 391 A.D. and reigned the country for 22 years.

During his regime, the king successfully prevented the invasion of Yen forces from Liao-tung in the north and at the same time sent his army to the south to fight back the Japanese troops. The epitaph of the monument shows that the king sent his troops four times to the south—in 396 A.D. for an expedition to Paekche, in 399 A.D. to demonstrate his military strength in the south, in 400 A.D. to help Silla and in 404 A.D. to have a naval battle with Japan.

The epitaph says that the king's first expedition to Paekche was indirectly aimed at driving the Japanese power behind Paekche out of the peninsula. The king brought his powerful naval forces to Paekche and took some 50 Paekche castles. When his forces approached the Paekche Metropolis after crossing the Han River, Paekche King surrendered. The second expedition to the south was to punish Paekche, which had maintained friendly relations with Japan in breach of its agreement with the king. During this expedition, Silla sent an envoy to the king's camp asking the king's help to get rid of the Japanese forces that had occupied Silla at that time. Thus, the third expedition to the south.

This time, the king led 50,000 soldiers to enter Silla and reached Kara, pursuing Japanese troops. The naval battle in 404 A.D. took place in the Tai-fang border on the west coast of the Central Peninsula which is believed to be off Inch'ŏn Bay.

That all these four expeditions had something to do with the Japanese forces shows how far Japanese power had reached in the peninsula at that time. Two most significant results of these expeditions were that the relationship between Koguryŏ and Silla was improved radically and that Paekche lost its power in the Han River area, which caused the country to move its capital to the south.

King Changsu, who succeeded King Kwanggaet'o, was on the throne for 79 years as his name (king longevity) indicates. He followed King Kwanggaet'o's policy and promoted the "Expansion to the South" project positively. The removal of the capital from Wan-tu to P'yŏngyang in 427 A.D. was highly significant in the process of the expansion-to-the-south-policy.

As a result of King Changsu's expedition to the south in 475 A.D., Paekche at last lost its capital Hansŏng, and moved the capital to Ungjin (now Kongju). Paekche had to move its capital again 60 years later from Ungjin to Soburi (now Puyŏ), which became the country's last capital.

In this regard, the history of Paekche can be divided into three as follows:

1. Hansŏng Era (Kwangju) (*350–475)
2. Ungjin Era (Kongju) (475–538)
3. Soburi Era (Puyŏ) (538–660)
   * Mark indicates estimated year.

Paekche's retreat to the south naturally influenced Japanese power in the peninsula. Every time Paekche moved down to the south, Japan ceded part of Kara to encourage Paekche to recover its power. Consequently, Japan lost most of the western half of Kara.

It must be noted, however, that Paekche's retreat to the south was not caused merely by Koguryŏ's invasion. Koguryŏ's invasion did constitute one of the major pressures from outside to force Paekche to move its capital to the south. But it is also true that Paekche itself had planned to move its capital to improve the country's administration and cultural system in an effort to recover its national prestige. And this was particularly true of the capital's removal to Soburi.

The most remarkable of Paekche's politico-military organization were the five *pu*'s of the capital and the five *pang*'s of local territories. The former—consisting of the Upper, Middle, Lower, Front and Rear *pu*'s—together designated five quarters of the capital, at the same time probably meaning five sections of the ruling class; the latter—Middle, Eastern, Southern, Western and Northern *pang*'s—were primarily military districts with some administrative functions.

Unlike Paekche, Silla maintained its metropolis in Kyŏngju from the beginning and achieved a gradual development of the conutry. Since the country was located very close to Kara, the conflicts with Kara always posed major diplomatic problems.

While Paekche expanded its territory into Kara, which was under Japan's control, in the form of agreed cession from Japan, Silla gradually invaded and amalgamated Kara

territory. Its invasion to Kara reached its peak during the
age of King Pŏphŭng, and was completed in the age of his
successor, King Chinhŭng in 562 A.D. King Chinhŭng's
"Monument of Territory Exploration," built in 561 A.D. in
Changnyŏng, Kyŏngsang-namdo, commemorates Silla's expansion into Kara.

Thus, the fall of Kara in 562 A.D. as the result of the
invasion by Paekche in the west and by Silla in the east,
meant the virtual end of Japan's control on the southern
part of the peninsula, and the beginning of the new era of a
tripartite struggle between Koguryŏ, Paekche and Silla.

It was about 170 years after Japan had battled with the
army of the King Kwanggaet'o that Kara perished. During
that 170 odd years, Paekche approached Japan to maintain
its power in the peninsula, while Silla strengthened its ties
with Koguryŏ to achieve its national development, though
there were some minor changes in their diplomatic policies
at times.

At the same time, Paekche exchanged friendly relations
with China's Southern Dynasties, while Silla and Koguryŏ
sought the support of the Northern Dynasties. In this respect, it can be said that the tripartite division of the peninsula at that time had some connection also with the struggle
between the Southern and Northern Dynasties of China.

8

PROSPERITY OF SILLA

The age of the tripartite division of the peninsula, thus
formulated, continued for about 100 years from then until
660 A.D. During this 100-year period, Koguryŏ maintained
its ambition to expand down to the south, but without much

success as in the cases of the Kings Kwanggaet'o and Changsu. Meanwhile, Paekche, which attempted to recover its national prestige by moving its metropolis three times, did actually restore its power temporarily and staged a series of attacks on Koguryŏ. But the most noteworthy change was that Silla gained an increasing power, cut its ties with Koguryŏ and even allied with Paekche to fight against Koguryŏ.

By the time Kara perished, Silla left the Koguryŏ camp and took a hostile attitude against Koguryŏ. The allied attack on Koguryŏ by Silla's King Chinhŭng and Paekche's King Sŏngmyŏng constituted the most serious blow to Koguryŏ. By this attack, Paekche occupied six provinces on the western coast while Silla took ten provinces on the eastern coast. Moreover, Silla later drove Paekche off the west coast area and established a province called Sinju centered on the Seoul district.

Silla's territorial expansion at that time was commemorated by the following three of the King Chinhŭng's monuments: (1) Maun Pass Monument at Maun Pass, Iwŏn County, Hamgyŏng-namdo; (2) Hwangch'o Pass Monument at Hwang-ch'o Pass, Hamhŭng County, Hamgyŏng-namdo, and (3) Pukhansan Monument at Pukhansan Peak, Kyŏnggi-do.

Silla's territorial expansion to both south and north— through the downstream of the Han River to the Inch'ŏn Bay, and through the downstream of the Naktong River to the Korean Strait—set a firm foundation for Silla's development thereafter. What, then, was behind Silla's so remarkable expansion at that time?

Silla was situated at the extreme south of the three countries on the peninsula at that time. While both Koguryŏ and Paekche set their capitals in the western part of the peninsula, Silla alone had its metropolis in the southern part of eastern Korea. It is now widely believed that the location of the Silla metropolis hampered the cultural development of the country, but few have noticed that the location itself contributed to the military expansion of the country. Silla had an ideal natural shape for defense against attack from outside, with its central district located in the plane alongside the Sŏch'ŏn River pouring into the Japan Sea, surrounded by mountains and hills. It had natural paths leading to north, south and west for traffic with the outside world. Thus, the country had the geographical shape of a natural fort, easy to defend and hard to attack. The configuration of the country was at the same time effective in maintaining the national solidarity and integrity of the people. Consequently, the clan system in Silla had a relatively smooth development.

Development of Silla was based upon the six-clan organization which had existed already at the time of its precursor Ch'en-han. By the time when the kingdom was solidly established, however, its six *pu*'s—Tok, Sadok, Ponp'l, Sŭppi, Chŏmdok and Hangi—had no longer been clans as they used to be, but were six political divisions of the ruling nobility instead. Later the names came to designate six quarters of Silla's royal capital. Reflection of the old *pu*'s is found also in the fact that the special district surrounding the capital, Kinae, was divided into six parts.

As for adoption of Chinese civilization, Silla lagged behind Paekche and Koguryŏ because of its geographical handicaps. However, the delay in importing Chinese civilization itself constituted an important condition for Silla's building up a firm foundation for a pure clan society of its own. In other words, Silla achieved a gradual cultural development, without having been spoiled by imported Chinese civilization. It was under such circumstances that Silla successfully attacked Koguryŏ, invaded Paekche and amalgamated Kara. After securing its opening to the sea in both south and west coast of the peninsula, Silla accelerated its traffic with China to import Chinese culture and to ally with China as a step toward conquering the whole peninsula.

Silla was the last of the three Korean countries to import Buddhism. It is generally believed that Buddhism found its way into Koguryŏ in 372 A.D. and into Paekche in 384 A.D. Although there are no definite data to prove when Buddhism was imported to Silla, existing documents show that it was in 527 A.D. that Buddhism was first authorized here. As for Koguryŏ and Paekche, there are no proofs to show when they gave official permission to profession of the religion.

At the time Buddhism was officially recognized in Silla, that country was positively expanding its territory toward the south and north, placing thousands of peoples of conquered land under its rule. In this regard, it may be safe to imagine that Silla took full advantage of Buddhism's universalism and class concept to give supreme authority to the king of Silla as the state reigning over the expanding nation.

9

CHINESE INVASIONS

Koguryŏ suffered a great setback from the prosperity of Silla and from Paekche's attack on its southern part. In addition, the unification of China's south and north dynasties by the Sui Emperor Wên-ti posed a serious threat to Koguryŏ from the north. Thus, Koguryŏ was not in a position to pay much attention to border troubles in the southern territory.

It goes without saying that Manchuria and Korea, situated to the northeast of China, have had a given strategical meaning to the situation in mainland China. When China was split into the Northern and Southern Dynasties, the northern power had to stabilize this northeastern area in order to maintain its security. Once China was unified, she needed the allegiance of Manchuria and Korea to check possible invasion by nomadic peoples from the north. Thus, China paid tremendous attention to political movement in this northeastern area.

It was only natural that the unification of China by the Sui Dynasty placed a strong psychological pressure on Koguryŏ, and that Koguryŏ felt a growing need to take defensive steps against Sui. Some of the historical documents show that Koguryŏ, in fear of invasion from Sui, concluded a joint defense agreement with Türk at that time. Türk was then a major power in northern Asia. It was by splitting Türk's power that Sui achieved the unification of China.

As soon as the unification of north and south China was achieved, Wên-ti, the Emperor of Sui, sent his envoy to Koguryŏ, demanding Koguryŏ's allegiance to Sui. Koguryŏ at once expressed its allegiance to Sui, but in 598 A.D. Koguryŏ invaded the Liao-hsi area with a lightening attack by the *Mo-ho* forces. In return, Wên-ti sent the Sui army and navy to defeat Koguryŏ, but without any sizable success, and withdrew its forces since the king of Koguryŏ apologized to save the face of Wên-ti. Six years later, the Emperor Wên-ti passed away, and the Koguryŏ problem was carried over untouched to the Emperor Yang-ti.

In 607 A.D., when Yang-ti visited the Türk Khan's court outside the Great Wall of China, he happened to witness a Koguryŏ envoy there. That was an apparent sign of Koguryŏ's alliance with Türk, Yang-ti understood, and he told the Koguryŏ envoy to ask the Koguryŏ king to visit Sui. This request was ignored by the king of Koguryŏ.

Thus, Yang-ti started preparations to attack Koguryŏ right away, and opened a war against Koguryŏ in 612 A.D. The war lasted for three years on an unprecedented scale, but narrowly fought back the Sui attack. Unable to shatter

Royal Mounds of Old Silla, Kyŏngju

Gold Crown, Old Silla

Stone Images,
the Cave Temple
Unified Silla

Sākyamuni

Brahman

Vajirapāni

Koguryŏ, the Emperor Yang-ti withdrew his army when Koguryŏ apologized.

The unsuccessful attack on Koguryŏ brought about a failure in Sui's control over the China mainland. As Türk rebelled against Sui in 618 A.D., Sui perished, and the Koguryŏ problem was again carried over unsettled to the T'ang Dynasty.

During the early days of the T'ang Dynasty, Koguryŏ, as well as Paekche and Silla, sent missions to T'ang to present tributes to the T'ang Emperor, ostensibly expressing their obedience to T'ang. In 642 A.D., however, Koguryŏ allied with Paekche to attack Silla, and almost succeeded in blocking the traffic route connecting Silla and T'ang. Thus, Silla called for T'ang's help. T'ai-tsung, the Emperor of T'ang, first sent envoys to Koguryŏ and Paekche in an attempt to stop their attack on Silla. But Koguryŏ ignored this. In 645 A.D., T'ang sent a strong army to Koguryŏ and attacked the An-shih Fortress on the bank of the Yalu River, but withdrew the army without a victory in the battle.

T'ang failed to defeat Koguryŏ in the second and third expeditions in 649 and 650 A.D. In the meantime, Paekche renewed its attack on Silla and took more than ten Silla castles. Thus, T'ai-tsung died before his goal of defeating Koguryŏ was half achieved, and the expedition to Koguryŏ was tentatively suspended.

T'ai-tsung's successor Kao-tsung, after a series of unsuccessful attacks on Koguryŏ, changed the original strategy and turned his target to Paekche. In 663 A.D., the T'ang ground and naval force of some 100,000, led by Commander-in-Chief Su T'ing-fang, reached the mouth of the Kŭm River by sea way, and went up the river to attack the Paekche metropolis of Puyŏ.

The City fell, and King Ŭija of Paekche surrendered himself to the T'ang forces. Commander-in-Chief Su T'ing-fang left part of his forces at the castle to guard the occupied

Paekche metropolis, and returned home with groups of Paekche prisoners of war, including King Ŭija. The inscription of the T'ang conquest of Paekche, carved on a large stone tower built in the suburbs of Puyŏ, is one of the detailed documents on this battle.

Encouraged by the successful conquest of Paekche, T'ang attacked Koguryŏ the following year. Su T'ing-fang's Army crossed the Yalu River and besieged P'yŏngyang. It was at this time that Kuisil Poksin and some other surviving retainers of Paekche united to restore Paekche and attacked the T'ang troops. Therefore, T'ang had to suspend the attack on Koguryŏ once again to subdue the Paekche rebels in Puyŏ. This was actually the last movement by the Paekche survived retainers to restore their country in the history of Paekche. A Paekche Prince, who had taken refuge in Japan, was called back to the country, and Japan rendered military help to Paekche's last effort to fight against the T'ang force in the Kŭm River area. But Japan's help was not successful, and the Paekche restoration movement ended up with total failure in 665 A.D.

After that, T'ang concentrated on a full-scale attack on Koguryŏ, and finally took the P'yŏngyang Castle and captured the king of Koguryŏ in 668 A.D. It was about seventy years after Wên-ti, the Emperor of Sui, first attacked Koguryŏ.

The continued effort by five noted emperors of Sui and T'ang to defeat Koguryŏ thus finally bore fruit. With Paekche having perished earlier, Silla unified the peninsula.

It is not too great an exaggeration to say that the situation in the Far East had never changed so radically in the history of the peninsula as at this time. Ever since the Lolang period, Koguryŏ had been aggressive against the northern part of China, and posed a strong obstacle to China's invasion to the east, as the country had a strong hold on Liao-tung, the Korean Peninsula and Southern Manchuria.

Koguryŏ as well as Silla and Paekche had taken a subordinate attitude to Chinese dynasties on the one hand, and maintained their national independence on the other hand. This attitude of political subjection to Chinese and other continental powers in order to maintain their relative independence was to become a traditional policy of all succeeding Korean dynasties.

10

UNIFICATION BY SILLA

T'ang sent its army to Koguryŏ and Paekche on the pretext of saving Silla from invasion by Koguryŏ and Paekche. As a result, Silla was asked by T'ang to offer its army to flank and back up the T'ang army at tremendous expense. The unification of the peninsula, which appeared to be achieved automatically by the fall of Paekche and Koguryŏ, was actually attributable to Silla's serious effort and expenses.

After the fall of the P'yŏngyang Castle, some surviving retainers of Koguryŏ rebelled against T'ang, as in the case of Paekche, and their leaders took refugee in Silla, which received them. Thus, Silla and T'ang became temporarily hostile to each other over the treatment of Koguryŏ rebel leaders. This hostility resulted in a six-year-long war between T'ang and Silla, but the war came to an end as T'ang's diplomatic policy became retrogressive and as Silla made an apology to T'ang.

As a result, T'ang's An-tung Regional Government at P'yŏngyang was moved to Liao-tung, and most part of the former Paekche and Koguryŏ land was placed under Silla's control in 675 A.D.

The Silla Dynasty lasted for 992 years under the reign of 56 kings. It is customary to divide the history of the Silla Dynasty into three major ages—Old Age, Middle Age and New Age.

Old Age—28 kings from King Hyŏkkŏse to King Chindŭk; 712 years

Middle Age—8 kings from King Muryŏl to King Hyegong; 127 years

New Age—20 kings from King Sŏndŭk to King Kyŏngsun; 156 years

Silla's prosperity reached its peak during the first 100 years after the unification of the peninsula was achieved.

Silla's conquest of Koguryŏ and Paekche and the consequent affiliation of their peoples were the most important national events for Silla after the amalgamation with Kara. Thus, Silla expanded and bolstered its social system.

Meanwhile, Silla expressed its obedience to T'ang by sending regular contributions to T'ang. As for Japan, Silla dispatched annual missions to present gifts to the Japanese emperor in a subordination similar to that toward T'ang.

Poems composed by Japanese diplomats and government officials who received Silla's missions at that time were included in *Kaifūsō*, which is believed to be the oldest collection of Sino-Japanese poetry, while those composed by Japanese envoys to Silla are recorded in *Man'yōshū*, the oldest collection of Japanese classical poetry.

However, the peaceful relationship between Silla and Japan did not last long. As Silla grew less subordinate to Japan, Japan mapped out a large-scale expedition to Silla, which, finally, was not realized. Silla stopped sending its official contribution mission to Japan at the time of King Hyegong.

On the other hand, Silla's relationship with T'ang grew increasingly closer. Silla's approach to Japan was not of a friendly nature from the beginning, because of its historical

hostility against Japan-supported Kara. Silla had kept sending contributions to Japan with the expectation that Japan
might be able to help Silla in the event Silla was attacked by
T'ang. After the T'ang Dynasty established a stable rule
over the whole of China, however, it was natural that Silla
gradually bolstered its ties with T'ang, partly because of the
cultural benefit.

Besides, the external environment at that time made the
relationship between the two countries closer, as Po-hai
which ruled Manchuria then tried to invade the northern
part of T'ang.

Silla, in its alliance with T'ang, played the role of check-
ing Po-hai from the east for T'ang, and in return T'ang
officially ceded the area south of the Taedong River to Silla.
Thus, Silla's territory at that time extended from the Taedong River at the northwestern end to the Anbyŏn-Wŏnsan
area in the south of Hamgyŏng-namdo in the northeastern
end. Silla divided the peninsula south of these northern
borders into nine circuits, and set capitals in five of these
nine states. Each of these circuits had counties under its
jurisdiction and each county had prefectures under it. This
is how Silla established its centralized authoritarian rule.
Names of the nine circuits, their respective capitals and the
number of administrative cities are as follows:

Nine Circuits	Five Capitals	Provinces	Counties
1. Sangju		10	30
2. Yangju	Kimhae	12	34
3. Kangju		11	27
4. Hanju	Chungwŏn	27	46
5. Sakchu	Pukwŏn	11	27
6. Myŏngju		9	25
7. Ungju	Sŏwŏn	13	29
8. Ch'ŏnju	Namwŏn	10	31
9. Muju		14	44

Relics and vestiges of Silla's at that time, left in the fields of Kyŏngju today, prove how deeply the T'ang culture were planted in Silla then.

But it can be imagined that the imported T'ang culture with its spiritual as well as material influence was enjoyed only by Silla's elite society, composed of royal families and nobles. The general public had little chance to partake in Silla's cultural development at that time. Therefore, it was natural that the elite society of Silla was the first to face the unfavorable consequence of the cultural development in Silla.

In any country of the world, the full maturity of a culture leads immediately to a period of decadence, and Silla was no exception. The growth of the central Government set up in the form of an imitation of T'ang's government system, as well as the establishment of centralized authoritative rule in Silla helped to raise the prestige of the dynasty and to make nobles grow wealthier. At the same time, however, the limitless desire of the nobles for pleasure and wealth caused degradation and corruption, which led to internal power struggles. These decadence phenomena came to the fore during the age of King Hyegong, about 100 years after Silla's unification of the peninsula. King Hyegong was killed by rebels and the Silla Dynasty came to a temporary end, marking the end of the Middle Age of Silla.

11

SILLA IN THE NEW AGE

King Sŏndŭk who succeeded King Hyegong had no direct blood relationship to King Muryŏl, though he was born in one of the royal families. Silla's New Age lasted for about 150 years, or about the same length of time as the Middle Age. However, as many as 20 kings came on to the throne during the period between King Sŏndŭk and the last king of the dynasty, King Kyŏngsun.

That the number of kings in the New Age was nearly three times as many as in the Middle Age indicates the short length of the reign of a king, and consequently the unstable rule of a king. In fact, a majority of the 20 kings in the New Age were killed by assassines or in civil wars. Bloody struggles over succession to the throne were witnessed between royal families during this period. The trouble inside the royal families naturally influenced the country's administration and its social life. While royal families were engaged in ugly struggles among themselves, national and regional politics were thrown into disorder.

In 822 A.D., Kim Hyŏnch'ang rebelled against the central Government in Ungju, now Kongju. After he took the area, he named it the Changan Kingdom and established his own era, Kyŏngun. His fathers' was one of the royal families which failed in the attempt to come to the throne. Kim Hyŏnch'ang expanded his power and temporarily occupied a vast area in southern Korea. Three years later, his son Pŏmmun attempted to establish himself at Yangju, near Seoul, but without success.

People in the southwestern coast of the Peninsula took advantage of the political disorder in the regional rule to pursue their individual interests in the East China Sea area, some of them as merchants and others as pirates. Among them was Chang Pogo (d. 841) who was engaged in three-way trade between Japan, Silla and T'ang by setting his base at Shan-tung Peninsula. He was later named Silla's Grand Commissioner of Ch'ŏnghae Defense Area (now Wando in Chŏlla-namdo). He was also known for curbing the outflow of Silla slaves to T'ang.

When the Silla Government stopped sending official missions to Japan, Silla merchants started private trade with Japan by merchant fleets. These merchant ships later became pirate ships that often invaded Kyūshū coast areas. Some of these merchants-pirates drifted to the Japan shores and asked for permission to settle down. These phenomena vividly reflected the political situation in Silla.

In spite of the political and social disorder in the late days of the New Age, Silla continued to send tributary missions to the T'ang court in an effort to keep its ties with T'ang intact. Silla kings of this era, most of whom acceded to the throne by illegal means, particularly needed the support of T'ang, and therefore raced to pay tributes to T'ang Emperors. These missions to T'ang were accompanied by an increasing number of priests and students. Therefore, a majority of Silla intellectuals in this era had the experience of studying in T'ang. The most well-known of all these Silla intellectuals was Ch'oe Ch'iwŏn. He entered T'ang at the age of twelve in about 868 A.D., and passed the Chinese civil service examination when he was twenty years old. After staying in T'ang for 18 years, he returned home and edited his official and private writings, made during his services as a Silla official in T'ang, into 20 volumes, and presented them to the Silla king. This work of his is entitled *Kyewŏn P'ŭil yŏng*, while a few other works of Ch'oe Ch'iwŏn are known to posterity. Some of his works written after his return to Silla, are left in the form of epitaphs or inscriptions. Unfortunately, Silla at that time was in so much disorder that his excellent works were not properly accepted. No details were known about the later years of his life, except that he died in retirement at Haein Temple in Mt. Kaya.

Soon after Ch'oe Ch'iwŏn returned to his home country, Silla entered the last days of political and social disorder with an increasing number of bandits and private armies rebelling against the central government. Of these rebels, Yang Kil who rose in arms at Pukwŏn (now Wŏnju), his follower Kung Ye, and Chin Hwŏn who established himself at Mujinju (Kwangju) were most powerful at that time.

Chin Hwŏn took Wansanju in 900 A.D. and later called himself the King of Hu-Paekche (Later Paekche). Kung Ye also called himself a king, set up a new state, Majin and set its capital in Ch'ŏlwŏn a year later, then set out on an expedition to the north. Kung Ye was assisted in his rebellion by his subordinate, Wang Kŏn, a native of Songak (Kaesŏng) who led a strong army and navy.

The state of Majin changed its name to T'aebong seven years later, but T'aebong perished in eight years because of Kung Ye's tyrannical rule. Then Wang Kŏn, with the support of his friends, founded a new state, Koryŏ. Thus, Silla, which was on the verge of collapse, was pitted against the two rising powers—Hu-Paekche in the southwest and Majin (T'aebong and later Koryŏ) in the northwest. This age in Korean history is called the Age of New or Later Three Kingdoms.

Chin Hwŏn was the first of all the rebel leaders to send his troops into Silla's capital. In 927 A.D., his troops raided the capital and forced the king of Silla to commit suicide. Kim P'u, one of the survivors of the Silla royal family, succeeded to the throne, to be called King Kyŏngsun. He tried secretly to ask Wang Kŏn, King of Koryŏ, for help in restoring Silla, but to no avail. In 935 A.D., he took refuge in Koryŏ. The King of Koryŏ received him politely, gave him the former Silla territory as his private dominion and had one of his daughters marry the former Silla King. Thus, the 992-year old Kingdom of Silla perished. A year later, Hu-Paekche, too, surrendered to Koryŏ, and the peninsula was once again unified by the hands of Koryŏ.

12

FOUNDING OF KORYO

It took about half a century for Wang Kŏn finally to unify the peninsula, after local warlords had begun expanding their power in their districts toward the end of the Silla period. Cities and villages in Korea were completely devastated. However, the transition of power from Kyŏngsun, the King of Silla, to Wang Kŏn, i.e. King T'aejo of Koryŏ, saw no bloodshed, which was very fortunate for the nation. Thus Koryŏ inherited the culture of Silla and on the basis of it developed its own culture incorporating several new elements.

While the capital of Silla was situated in the southeastern part of the peninsula, Koryŏ set up its seat in the central part of the peninsula near the estuary of the Yesŏng River on the west coast, convenient for marine transportation. This selection of the capital site helped the development of the northern part of the peninsula which until then was unexploited. The part north of P'yŏngyang stretched beyond the frontier of Korea and until then was left as hunting ground for the Tungusic peoples of Manchuria. As soon as he assumed power, T'aejo made concerted efforts to develop the northern wilderness by designating P'yŏngyang as the Western Capital, whence he even planned moving the seat of his government at one time. The scheme to open up the north was succeeded by kings in the following generations.

But this northward march by the Koreans met opposition from the northern powers. The Koreans had to fight three big powers that tried to expand into the peninsula—first, Kitais (Liao) which had destroyed the Po-hai Kingdom, then Jurchins (Chin) and finally Mongols (Yüan). One of the reasons for these northern nations' march into Korea is believed to be their attempt to secure resources which were scarce in their native areas. But a more important reason undoubtedly was that they wanted Koryŏ in the east subdued in the pursuit of their common southward march to capture China. Indeed, on occasion they attempted to attack South China from the sea by crossing the neck of the peninsula and going into the sea from the southwest coast of Korea. Actually, Koryŏ did have relations with South China that justified such attention from the northern powers.

Wang Kŏn came from Kaesŏng. Legend about his ancestors contains stories of trade with China and in the days when Wang Kŏn worked as a general of Kung Ye, he led the navy to put the sea south of the peninsula under his control. Together with the fact that there were many with the family name of Wang among the Sillans who sent envoys to South China toward the end of the Silla period, these records lead us to presume that Wang Kŏn might have been one of marine merchants who were active in the East China Sea at that time.

Both Hu-Paekche and Taebong of Kung Ye had relations with South China but neither established ties as firm as Wang Kŏn did. He frequently dispatched emissaries to the Latter-T'ang Dynasty in North China as soon as he assumed the sovereignty of Koryŏ and was later officially granted the title of King of Koryŏ by the Chinese and adopted the Chinese era. After the Latter T'ang Dynasty fell, the Koryŏ ruler formed ties with Latter Chin, Latter Han, and Latter Chou, (known as the kingdoms of the Five Dynasties Period in North China) one after another and then developed relations with the Sung Dynasty which unified China. After Koryŏ came under the influence of the Manchurian powers, it did everything to retain its ties with Sung, which in turn invited added oppression from the Manchurian powers.

The culture of Koryŏ can be said to be a hybrid developed on the basis of the Silla culture and by the addition of the Chinese Sung culture. The first 60 years of Koryŏ, when it had free contact with the Five Dynasties and the Sung Dynasty—before the interference from Manchuria, was the period during which the foundation of Koryŏ was laid.

In the early years of Wang Kŏn's rule, he seemed to have followed the old system of Silla and placed most emphasis on the welfare of the people. Although most of the officials in his court must have been those who had served in the Silla court, there were also Chinese who actively worked in Wang's court and drafted policies for Koryŏ. For instance, the first civil service examination in Koryŏ was enforced on the recommendation of Shuang Chi (Sang Kŭi) who came from China accompanying an official envoy of Latter Chou. This new examination system is said to have promoted academism in Koryŏ. It was during the reign of King Sŏngjong that both the central and local government organizations of Koryŏ were reformed and strengthened. The new structure was mostly a faithful copy of the Chinese system.

Under this drastically reformed system of Sŏngjong, local districts were divided into ten circuits and were governed by twelve provincial military governors. This set up was reorganized into the five provinces and two territories after a couple of changes.

Sŏngjong, when he acceded to the throne, not only reformed the governmental organizations, as mentioned above, but also strove to rule justly through various means such as by soliciting the opinions of chief vassals on problems of administration. The most famous among views presented by the retainers was the 28-point recommendation of Ch'oe Sŭngno. It was very significant that Ch'oe started his recommendation with the defense of the northwest, as most of the major external difficulties for Koryŏ came from that direction.

13

EXTERNAL TROUBLES AND RISE
OF THE YIS AND THE CH'OES

Ch'oe Sŭngno had in mind none other than the tremendous powers in Manchuria when he urged Sŏngjong to strengthen the defense on the northwestern frontier. In the age of Silla, the power in Manchuria was Po-hai situated along the Hūrha River. Silla and Po-hai were not hostile although the two were not specially friendly.

Po-hai was destroyed by Kitai in 926 A.D., within several years after Wang Kŏn's accession to the throne, and its subjects fled to Korea in great numbers. Kitai, which rose in Western Manchuria along the Shira Müren River, captured Inner and Outer Mongolia, moved southward aiming at the heart of China, and by the time the Sung Dynasty was established, its advance guard had the northern part of the present Hopei and Shansi Provinces under its influence.

Between these fast growing Kitai and Koryŏ, there existed a wild land where the Jurchin tribe had settled. The development of the north launched by Koryŏ, as mentioned earlier, was begun by pacifying the tribesmen. Kitai did the same, and when the Manchurian power reached the western bank of the Yalu River, Koryŏ's development had reached the opposite bank from the south. The two powers were to clash there. The direct cause of the conflict was the question of power and control over the Jurchin tribe. But in addition, it was necessary for Kitai to subdue Koryŏ in order to put pressure on Sung.

Koryŏ was first invaded and partly controlled by Kitai in 994 A.D. Thereafter, the Manchurian power moved down into the peninsula from time to time to further the invasion, and in 1011 A.D., Kitai troops captured the capital, forcing King Hyŏnjong to southward flight.

Tŭkjong, who succeeded Hyŏnjong as king, took advantage of a civil war in Kitai to strengthen his country's defense, and built a long fortress along the northern border. The fortress, which took 12 years to complete, stretched clear across the peninsula, one end on the Yalu River banks, and the other near Chŏngp'yŏng, Hamgyŏng-namdo. Remains of this great engineering work can still be seen today.

The reign of Hyŏnjong, which can be called the first trouble-ridden period of Koryŏ, gave birth to an epoch-making cultural achievement: the first printing of the complete Buddhist Tripitaka. One of the motives that promoted this great work, which took more than 60 years to complete, must have been the attempt by the rulers to resort to the power of merit thus accumulated to turn back the invaders. This religious work was perfected when Monk Ŭich'ŏn, titled Taehak Kuksa, of royal birth, edited and printed a supplementary series to the Tripitaka devoting his entire life to it. Ŭich'ŏn, by the time of his death in 1101 A.D., had gathered as many as 4,740 volumes of Buddhist scriptures to complete the collection. The second period of trouble for Koryŏ began shortly after this great religious work was accomplished.

The long fortress, whose construction was started in the reign of Tŭkjong and completed in that of Chŏngjong, had the double role of defending Koryŏ from the Kitai invaders and turning back the Jurchin tribesmen in the northern part of the peninsula. At that time, Jurchins were divided into two groups. One centered in the present Hamgyŏng-do and the other along the Sungari River. In the reign of the Sukchong, the northern Wan-yen Tribe emerged victorious, put the southern tribes under its control and posed a great threat to Koryŏ from the north. In an attempt to forestall the growing power in the north, Koryŏ sent forces to subdue the Jurchin Tribes. More than 100,000 Koryŏ troops under the command of Yun Kwan seized the fortress of Chŏng-p'yŏng, captured the Hamgyŏng plain and returned home triumphantly after building nine fortresses in the plain.

However, the defeated Jurchin were determined to take revenge and after a few years, succeeded in recapturing the plain and seizing the nine fortresses. Some years later, A-pao-chi, chief of the Wan-yen Tribe unified his people and ⟨of Jürchen⟩ built a strong nation, naming it Chin (1115 A.D.). He looked for opportunities to march south and destroy Kitai, and for that purpose, tried to establish friendly relations with Sung and Koryŏ.

Finding a common objective in beating Kitai, Chin and Sung formed a united front and launched a joint attack on the enemy. They finally destroyed Kitai in 1125 A.D. But as soon as their common enemy was removed, each found a new adversary in the other, and sought a pledge of alliance from Koryŏ.

Having experienced a similar dilemma at the hands of Kitai, Koryŏ this time managed to pledge obedience to the two powers and conducted a calculating two-front diplomacy. Added to this external trouble was a crisis within, created by the rising influence of the Yis, relatives of the king, and the expansion of power by military leaders over civil officials.

The period of about 100 years from Chŏngjong to Injong saw Koryŏ's national power reach a peak and its culture attain a level of unprecedented height with great works produced in the fields of literature, art and handicraft and religion. During this time of national prosperity, the Koryŏ sovereigns were placed in a precarious position because of the threat from Yi Chayŏn, who came from K'yŏngwŏn (present Inch'ŏn) and had became influencial in the court as a distant relative of the king. The original relationship was built in the reign of Munjong, when Yi's daughters were made the queens of the sovereign. One of the queens gave birth to Sunjong, Sŏnjong and Sukchong who in succession became the kings of Koryŏ. Furthermore, Yi Chagyŏm, one of Chayŏn's grandsons, had his two daughters marry King Injong, who was his nephew, to strengthen his family's control over the court. Chagyŏm held both the military and civil command by acting as the guardian of the king. There was nothing his family hoped for that they could not get.

The king and his retainers finally broke loose from the control of the despotic administrator and plotted against him. The angered Chagyŏm killed many of his opponents and set the palace afire but finally was arrested and banished to an island, thus ending the long prosperity of the Yis.

Following the usurpation of the Yi, Monk Myoch'ŏng revolted, opening the way for generals and military leaders, who until then had little power in the court, to gain more influence. Some of the generals such as Chŏng Chungbu soon gained the power to enthrone and dethrone the king, thus heading the military leaders' rise to influence in the court.

Another general to rise to the highest position in the court was Ch'oe Chunghŏn, who laid the foundation for the exclusive power exercised by his descendants for four generations. The extent of his influence can be well imagined from the fact that he enthroned four kings and dethroned two. Ch'oe made his private home the administrative office and called in civil and military officers to give them orders. This is called the *Tobang* administration.

When Ch'oe Chunghŏn died and his power was inherited by his son Ch'oe I in 1219 A.D., serious external trouble developed for Koryŏ with the Mongols.

Mongolian
Warriors

One Page of Chinese
Tripitaka,
Koryŏ Edition

Celadon Graze,
Late 14th Century

14

MOVING THE CAPITAL
TO KANGHWA

Before Ch'oe Chunghŏn died, the Mongols had become a great empire under Chinggis Khan who unified the nation and made himself the Emperor of the Mongols in ceremonies by the Onon River (1206 A.D.). When Ch'oe I assumed power, the growing influence of the powerful empire reached the border of Koryŏ.

First, trouble came indirectly through the surviving forces of Kitai defeated by Chin and the Mongols, who crossed the Yalu River in the northern territory of Koryŏ and wrought havoc there. Koryŏ managed to suppress the Kitai troops at Fort Kangdong in P'yŏngan-namdo in 1218 A.D. with the help of the Mongols and the Jurchin Kingdom of Tung-chen then situated along the Tuman River. But in return for the assistance it received, Koryŏ had to pledge its brotherhood with these two powers and to pay annual tributes.

After Chinggis Khan died and Ögödei Khan succeeded him, the Mongols moved to subdue Koryŏ as well as Chin. Powerful forces were sent into the peninsula to besiege the capital, Kaegyŏng, in 1231 A.D. King Kojong found no way out but to surrender. He accepted control by the Mongols by receiving *darughachis* or governors as the administrative heads for each local administrative district including the capital.

Immediately after the Mongol troops left Koryŏ, the Koryŏ Government took a drastic measure to cope with the precarious situation by moving the capital to Kanghwa Island, southeast of Kaegyŏng. The king moved to the new capital in July, 1232 A.D. to launch a new era.

The transfer of the capital appears to have been quite effective for its original purpose—to secure the safety of the royal family from invaders. However, when the king's position in the politics of Koryŏ at that time is considered, this step can also be interpreted as having actually been planned by Ch'oe I to ensure the safety of his administration.

Moving the seat of the government to an island proved effective in escaping the persuing Mongols because the invaders had little marine power and were unable to attack the island. The life of the people on the island was safely maintained by transporting food, collected tax and other necessary materials from the southern part of the peninsula by sea. However, this assurance of the security of the rulers of Koryŏ was secured at the price of their subjects, as the angered Mongols took the moving of the capital as symbolic of the resistance of the king. Consequently the invaders intensified their persecution of the Koryŏ people on the peninsula, and the safety of the ruling class now in a self-imposed exile in the Kanghwa Island was protected at the cost of their subjects left behind.

After Ch'oe I, the central planner of the capital transfer, died in the court on the island, the Koryŏ Government softened its attitude toward the Mongols and at one time compiled with the long standing demand of the Mongols to leave the island and submit by building a new palace on the land opposite the island.

However, Ch'oe Hang, who succeeded Ch'oe I, reversed the policy before long and strengthened the island capital's defenses, showing his determination to stay on the island. The offended Mongols increased their troops in Koryŏ and went through the catalog of outrages on the peninsula leaving it in complete ruins.

In time, Ch'oe Hang died after ill health and his son

Ch'oe Ŭi was assassinated, ending four generations of tyranny by the Ch'oes. With the fall of the Ch'oes the policy toward the Mongols underwent a complete change and the king pledged to the invaders that he would move the capital back to Kaegyŏng and send his son to the Mongolian court to pay his respects to the Emperor. The Prince left for Mongolia in April of 1259 A.D., 28 years after the capital was transferred to the island. In the same year, as the fortresses on the island were being torn down under the supervision of Mongolian officials, the king died on the island.

King Kojong's life, which ended tragically, was a continuous hardship brought about by the Mongolian invasion and usurpation of power by the Ch'oes. But during his reign culture on the Korean Peninsula developed greatly. As mentioned earlier, the first complete Buddhist Tripitaka in Korea was engraved on wood for printing during the eras of Hyŏnjong and Munjong. These engraved blocks were destroyed by the Mongolian troops at the Puin Temple outside the present Taegu where they were stored. This occured in the year king moved to the island. Attempting to resort to the merit of the pious deed in turning back the invaders, King Kojong started several years later engraving the collection anew on wood blocks and ordered the engravers mostly in the relatively rich Chŏlla-namdo to do the job. The work was accomplished after 16 years of toil, and the engraved blocks are kept today at the Haein Temple in Kyŏngsang-namdo as cultural treasures most highly valued as old Buddhistic documents.

Although the walls of the island capital were destroyed and reconstruction was started on the old capital of Kaegyŏng, high officials of Koryŏ would not immediately move back to the old center of administration. The officials, including Kim Chun, Im Yŏn and his son, who were successively in power after the falls of the Ch'oes, had found the defunct island capital a comfortable place to live and from which to wield their arbitrary political power after 30 years of settlement.

It was not until 1271 A.D., 10 years after the prince returned from the visit to Mongolia and was enthroned as King Wŏngjong, that the administrative center was officially moved to Kaegyŏng from the Island.

King Wŏnjong was able to hold administrative power in his hands, as rebellious vassals were either killed or already dead when he moved to the new capital. But he found his country under the iron grip of the Mongols as their subject state. The first role his country was given by the Mongolians was to provide the way for the Mongols' contact with Japan and later to serve as a supply center for great numbers of Mongol troops who marched down the peninsula on their way to attack Japan.

15

KORYO AND THE MONGOLIAN INVASION OF JAPAN

Emperor Khubilai of Yüan (Mongol), who acceded to the throne after Möngke Khan died just about the same time as Kojong's death, before long softened the attitude toward Koryŏ, as he was preparing to wage an all-out offensive against Sung China in the south. The softened attitude is best seen in Khubilai's immediate releasing of the prince of Koryŏ from his capital at the news of the death of King Kojong and making him the new king.

Khubilai then saw a more positive way to utilize Koryŏ in his war with Sung: to attack Sung from the sea making use of the Koryŏ fleet. In time, the Yüan Emperor found another role in Koryŏ, as he learned from the Koreans about Japan's situation in the sea east of Koryŏ, and attempted to open contacts with Japan. In 1266 A.D., the first emissary of Yüan to Japan arrived in Koryŏ.

At that time, Japan did not have official diplomatic relations with either Sung or Koryŏ but had close and active contacts, as the three seafaring countries engaged in trade. They also exchanged envoys on many occasions such as when sending back seamen of each other's country who were saved after meeting accidents on the sea. Some Japanese traders made contracts with their Korean counterparts who saw ships annually sent to Kimju (Kimhae). Koryŏ received these traders from Japan in a specially built guest house. Thus there was every reason for Yüan to give special attention to Japan in her relations with Koryŏ, in view of Japan's strategic importance within a scheme to conquer the South Chinese Dynasty.

Unwilling to help Yüan make contacts with Japan, Koryŏ was most reluctant to serve as a guide to the Yüan emissary in his trip to Japan. Anyway, the Mongolian envoy finally reached Japan and conveyed Khubilai's intention to make the island country a subject of Yüan. Meeting with a Japanese refusal, Yüan dispatched strong invading forces to Japan twice, in 1274 and 1281 A.D., only to suffer disasterous defeats. Details of these two campaigns will not be mentioned here; instead, let us see what a heavy burden Koryŏ had to bear in helping Yüan attack Japan.

Five years after Yüan started preparations to conquer Japan, in 1270 A.D. she took over the Koryŏ territory north of the Chabi Mountains and made the Western Capital (P'yŏngyang) Tung-ning-fu, a Mongolian city, to serve as a base for the eastward invasion. This was made possible for the Mongols as Ch'oe T'an, a high Koryŏ official at P'yŏngyang, rebelled against the king and surrendered to Yüan; it just met the Mongolian purpose to set up an operational center on the peninsula for the battles against both Japan and Sung. It was not until after 1290 A.D. that the northern part of the peninsula was recovered by Koryŏ.

Then Yüan set up outposts in eleven areas of Koryŏ including Kaegyŏng, P'yŏngyang and Kimju, by dispatching 5,000 troops. This also was to prepare for the invasion of Japan.

When Yüan finally decided to subjugate Japan by force, the burden on Koryŏ became heavier. For the first invasion attempt of Yüan, some 35,000 Koryŏ workers were mobilized to build more than 900 vessels to transport the Mongol troops across the Tsushima Strait. The boats were built at Pyŏnsan and Ch'ŏngwansan of Chŏlla-namdo. For the first attack, Yüan sent a total of 26,000 soldiers of which 6,000 were Koryŏ men, 5,000 were Yüan troopers already stationed at various outposts on the peninsula and the rest were Yüan and Sung naval forces. They all marched down the peninsula and boarded the Koryŏ-built vessels at Happ'o (present Masan) for Japan.

The first invasion ended in failure. After destroying Sung in 1279 A.D., the Mongols again attempted to capture the island country in the east in the following year, this time with much greater forces.

For the second invasion, Yüan sent forces via two routes, one through the same course as the first invading forces, and the other via the sea route from a port of Sung in South China which the Mongols just captured. The first group, the East Course forces, were made of 40,000 soldiers including 10,000 Koreans, who sailed for the Southern Koryŏ port to Japan aboard 900 vessels which also were built by Koreans. The other, the South Marine forces, were composed of 100,000 Yüan soldiers who sailed in 1,500 vessels. These powerful invading forces again failed and Yüan gave up her attempt to capture Japan.

During the 16 years in preparation for the two unsuccessful Yüan attempts at the invasion of Japan, Koryŏ became impoverished, since she had had to supply soldiers, vessels, non-fighting personnel such as steersmen, and foodstuffs for the Yüan forces.

King Wŏnjong died three months before the first Mongol invading forces left for Japan. His son, Sim, was in the Yüan Court and had just taken a daughter of the Mongol Emperor as his bride. Khubilai told Sim to return Koryŏ and accede to the throne of Koryŏ.

Thus after Sim was enthroned as King Ch'ungnyŏl, the bond of Koryŏ's subordination to Yüan established in the reign of Wŏnjong became stronger and four succeeding Kings of Koryŏ were married to women of the Yüan Imperial family. It is believed that these marriages not only made the Koryŏ royal family a close relative of the Yüan sovereign but also had wider impact on various phases of social life in Koryŏ. The spreading of Mongolian fashion in people's dress was one instance of such an impact; language also did not escape Mongolian influence and many Mongolian words are believed to have entered the Koryŏ vocabulary then. All told, Koryŏ was placed under Mongolian control for nearly a century.

16

FROM KORYO TO CHOSON

As Koryŏ-Yüan relations became stabilized (as mentioned above) after the second unsuccessful Yüan invasion of Japan, Kings of Koryŏ became alienated from the actual administrative power, although in different implication from that in the Kanghwa Island capital age. For, quite frequently, the kings lived in Peking instead of at their palace in Kaegyŏng, and sent directives from the Mongolian capital, by which their men managed home affairs.

Under such political circumstances, the welfare of the general public was scarcely promoted. Adding to the trouble was the rampancy of Japanese seamen who often turned into pirates and attacked coastal areas of Koryŏ.

After they turned back the Yüan invasion, the Japanese accelerated their trade with foreign countries and at times, the seamen and traders resorted to violence when they failed to conduct profitable trade. (The guest house for the Japanese traders established in Kimju was abolished after the Mongolian attack on Japan.)

The first mention of these Japanese acts of violence was found in Korean historical documents as early as the reign of Kojong before the capital was moved to Kanghwa. However, it was about 50 years after the second Mongolian invasion of Japan that the Japanese seamen-traders began seriously terrorising the Koreans. Districts south of Kyŏnggi-do suffered annually at the hands of the rampaging Japanese and, as Koryŏ exiles began joining the Japanese to serve as guides, the damages began to spread further inland from the coastal areas. The pirates attacked and captured rice storing centers on land and seized vessels loaded with tax rice on the sea.

As there were little resistance to check the violent Japanese pirates, they grew each year in power and inflicted increased damages on Koryŏ people. The trouble was increased when some Koreans copied the Japanese invaders and ransacked many communities disguised as Japanese. Thus, how to defend the nation against the pillage of the Japanese pirates became the prime problem for kings in the late years of Koryŏ since King Kongmin.

When Kongmin acceded to the throne, Mongol power finally began receding on the continent and the Chinese revolted against the Mongol rule in many parts. Strongest among the rebelling Chinese was Chu Yüan-chang who rose to power along the Yangtze River, moved to Chin-ling or the present Nanking, and finally marched northward to capture the Yüan capital now Peking. The defeated Yüan forces and people, headed by Emperor Shun-ti, fled north to settle in K'ai-p'ing in Inner Mongolia.

Prior to the enthronement of Chu Yüan-chang as the Emperor of Ming China at Nanking in 1368 A.D., King Kongmin of Koryŏ took advantage of the declining power of Yüan, and several years after acceding to the throne, marched north to recover Koryŏ territory in Hamgyŏng-do. He then crossed the Yalu River to pose as though he were ready to advance further northwestward but, upon receiving envoys from Ming, he accepted the Chinese bid and pledged obedience to Ming.

In contrast to his earlier years, Kongmin indulged in mal-administration in the latter half of his reign, took a priest called Pyŏnjo into his confidence and followed whatever advice the priest gave. Finally, the retainers mutinied against the king and killed first the priest and then the king (1374 A.D.). Kongmin's son U was made the new king at the age of ten, supported by Yi Inim.

Yüan based in K'ai-p'ing recovered its power in time, began a southward march toward Ming and asked Koryŏ's alliance, sending envoys to Kaegyŏng one after another. The vassals of King U were divided equally between those who sided with Ming and those who favored alliance with Yüan.

As the Liao-tung area was thrown into confusion because of the arrival of Ming's advance troops there to meet Yüan forces, Ch'oe Yŏng, the leader of the pro-Yüan group in the Koryŏ court, dispatched forces to attack Ming outposts in Liao-yang. However, Gen. Ch'o Minsu and Gen. Yi Sŏnggye who commanded the forces on order from Ch'oe Yŏng, were against offending Ming and halted the troops on an island in the Yalu River instead of storming the Ming bases. The generals sent letters to Ch'oe Yŏng arguing that antagonizing Ming was not in the interest of Koryŏ. When Ch'oe Yŏng refused to accept their stand, the generals turned their forces to Kaegyŏng, took the capital over, executed the pro-Yüan leader, and dethroned King U to make his son Ch'ang the new king.

When, before long, a plot to restore U to the throne was exposed, Yi Sŏnggye, who then wielded most influence, dethroned Ch'ang and made Yo the new king, called King Kongyang. After this, Yi expanded his power rapidly until finally he removed all opposition and dethroned King Kongyang to make himself the king of Koryŏ with the backing of his aides. This was in 1392 A.D.

Immediately after acceding to the throne, Yi dispatched an envoy to Ming and asked for recognition. Upon winning Ming's approval, Yi Sŏnggye changed the name of the state to Chosŏn, and moved the capital from Kaegyŏng to Hanyang, the present Seoul, to lay the foundation for his rule. Winning Ming's recognition was necessary not as a diplomatic measure but as an internal political tool for strengthening his position. Although Yi Sŏnggye won the approval of Ming as the king of Chosŏn, it was not until his grandson T'aejong became the king that an official seal of the king was given by the Chinese emperor, formally confirming Korea's status as a tributary of Ming.

17

PROBLEMS IN THE SOUTH AND THE NORTH

To understand the history of the 500-year-long reign of

the Yi Dynasty, we must know the life of the founder of the dynasty. Yi Sŏnggye, T'aejo of Chosŏn, was born at Haek-sok-ri, Yŏnghŭng, Hamgyŏng-namdo. There were three factors that paved the way for his eventual rise to the throne. The first was that his family since the days of his grandfather had lived in Hamgyŏng-do. The second was that he was a brilliant general and made himself known by distinguished services in the victorious campaigns against the Jurchins in the north and in the defense against the Japanese pirates. The third and the most important factor was that he unified the Koryŏ administration which was split over which, Ming or Yüan, the country should take side with. As mentioned earlier, Yi Sŏnggye was dispatched to attack a Ming outpost but realized the disadvantage of antagonizing Ming, turned his forces to expel the pro-Yüan group from the Koryŏ court and assumed the ruling position in the administration. He then became king through the arrangements he made, which took the appearance of King Kongyang's voluntarily vacating the throne for Yi to take it.

The reason why his birth place was important was that the area where he was born was traditionally outside the Koryŏ territory, and in the area of the projected northern development of Koryŏ. While northern expansion was successful in the western half (P'yŏngan-do) and the Koryŏ development efforts reached to the left bank of the Yalu River, it did not make much progress in the eastern part (Hamgyŏng-do). The northern end of the development reached no farther than Ch'ŏllyŏng (the northern boundary of Kangwŏn-do) at one time, and at another time, it moved to the long fortress outside Chŏngp'yŏng. During the Jurchin campaign, the Koryŏ forces occupied the Hamgyŏng plain for a few years only to be driven out by Jurchins again. The Yis had settled in this area which was under the influence of Jurchins.

The Yis began serving the Koryŏ court when Sŏnggye's

father came to assist King Kongmin, who tried to expand his power taking advantage of the falling influence of Yüan. For this service, Sŏnggye's father was granted a high military rank, opening the way for his son's rise in Koryŏ. Sŏnggye followed up with meritorious services in the suppression of Jurchins, though ironically, he inherited the brave spirit of Jurchin tribesmen.

One of the important roles the Yi Dynasty played in the history of Korea was that it definitely integrated the northern districts of Hamgyŏng-do and P'yŏngan-do into the territory of Korea. This would not have been possible without the particular geographical background of the Yis. This northern expansion was completed after 50 years of effort, when King Sejong set up the six fortresses of Ch'angsŏng, Hoenyŏng, K'yongwŏn, K'yonghung, Onsŏng and Punyŏng in the eastern half of the new territory south of the Tumen River, and established the four provinces of Much'ang, Uye, Chasŏng and Yŏyŏn in the west at the upper reaches of the Yalu River.

Upon acceding to the throne, T'aejo took further measures to defend the country against Japanese piracy as a natural consequence of his successful defensive operations. The best and the most drastic measure against attack by pirates was to have them caught at their departing ports by the ruler of that country. Asking the Japanese authorities to control the lawless seamen had been done before him, but not as positively and earnestly as T'aejo did. Immediately after he became king, T'aejo sent an envoy of goodwill to the Japanese Government of Ashikaga Shogunate, and asked its favor in prohibiting piracy. At the same time, he dispatched troops to Kyŏnggi-do, Kyŏngsang-do and Chŏlla-do while encouraging desertion of pirates by providing the deserters with stable jobs.

In 1399 A.D., Korea concluded an official amity agreement with the Shogunate, opening the way for an exchange of emissaries on various occasions. From the Japanese side, missions visited Korea frequently to obtain complete sets of Buddhist Tripitaka. These missions were headed by Buddhist priests who were accorded the utmost courtesy at the royal capital (Seoul). Some of the suite members were given permission to conduct trade with Korea.

The Korean Government's friendly policy toward Japan was not limited to official relations. The government encouraged free trade between the two nations by providing maximum conveniences to Japanese private citizens, with the result that even those who had engaged in smuggling and piracy turned to legitimate, peaceful trade. Korea-Japan trade expanded so much in time, that in the reign of Sejong, regulations about trade came to be established. Trade ports were limited to Naeip'o (Ungch'ŏn), Pusanp'o (Pusan) and Yŏmp'o in Kyŏngsang-do, an annual quota of trading ships was set and official procedures for visitors were laid. This situation lasted until the Sō Family, feudal lord of Tsushima, concluded an agreement with Korea in 1443 A.D. to monopolize the right to trade with Korea.

To add a few later developments, the Sō Family continued to enjoy a monopolistic position as Japanese. People needed the Sō's introduction to visit Korea. In 1510 A.D., after Tsushima people in the three trading ports of Korea expanded their influence, the Sō Family had a disagreement with Korea over trade expansion and sent forces to Naeip'o, joined by dissident Tsushimans in the three ports. This is known as the Revolt of the Three Ports.

The contacts between Tushima and Korea were suspended as a result of the incident but were reopened in the following year after a series of negotiations. As a punitive measure, Korea closed Pusanp'o and Yŏmp'o, leaving only Naeip'o for the Sō Family to trade with. Another disagreement developed between the Korean residents in Naeip'o and Tsushimans about 30 years later, which resulted in the moving of the trading port from Naeip'o to Pusan.

Along with the settlement of external troubles, internal problems in Korea were steadily solved, laying the foundation for prosperity and great cultural achievements.

18

LITERARY ACTIVITIES

Together with other achievements, great cultural accomplishments mark Sejong's region. The later period of Koryŏ which preceded the Yi Dynasty was chaotic as far as the political order was concerned, but was quite active in the cultural field. This was attributable to the frequent exchanges with Peking, the capital of Yüan, where quite a number of Chinese scholars of Southern Sung had settled. The new achievements in philosophy and other studies which Koryŏ intellectual leaders learned through contact with the Chinese scholars, gave a great impetus to promotion of scholarship in Koryŏ citizens to take civil service examinations and giving official posts to successful students.

Many of the scholars of the late Koryŏ era continued to take responsible positions in the cultural field in the early Yi Dynasty days. These scholars wrote or compiled many books of importance in the first half century of the dynasty. Let us dwell here on a few great works in the field of official annals and history.

First comes the *Yi Dynasty Annals*. Compiling records of the life and achievements of a king after he died was started in the early days of Koryŏ, following the Chinese custom. The annal of T'aejo was first compiled by Ha Yun and other scholars in the reign of King T'aejong and was later revised

but not
done
continuous
until Yi

by Chŏng Inji and others in the late years of Sejong, while those of the second King Chŏngjong and third sovereign T'aejong were completed in 1419 A.D. under the reign of Sejong. With the compilation of the annals of the first three sovereigns of the Yi Dynasty, detailed situations surrounding the creation of the dynasty and the spirit in which it was founded were recorded and relayed to later generations.

The compilation of annals continued thereafter as an important task of each generation until the last sovereign of the dynasty. Furthermore, annals were made in four copies, either hand written or printed, and kept in the special historical libraries at Sŏngju, Ch'ŏnju and Chungju in addition to the one in the capital; later, the number of copies was increased to five and they were placed in libraries at the capital, Kanghwa, T'aepaek-san of Kyŏngsang-pukto, O'tae-san of Kangwŏn-do, and Chŏksang-san of Chŏlla-pukto. These annals, totalling about 1,700 volumes, have served later historians as the fundamental materials for studying the history and institutions of the dynasty.

Equally important was the compilation of the history of the 470 year-long Koryŏ. The work was started as early as the reign of T'aejo, and, after half a century of continuous efforts, it finally materialized in the form of two books, one a 139-volume *Koryŏ-sa* in 1451 A.D., another a 35-volume *Koryŏ-sa, Chŏlyo* in the following year, both important historical sources of great value. That the histories of the preceding period were compiled immediately after the new dynasty was born was most fortunate for the preservation and classification of the previous era's documents and books. Part of the intention behind compiling *Koryŏ-sa* was apparently an effort to put on record the position of the new dynasty on the events that led to the founding of the new state, *Koryŏ-sa* is valuable not only for historical facts but also for the thinking and philosophy of the founders of the new dynasty it recorded.

Next comes *Chiriji* (Geographical Gazetteer) compiled
also in the reign of Sejong. The compilation of the geographical gazetteer, which provides the fundamental practical
information for administration, was started in 1424 A.D.
and was first completed by Yun Hoe, Sin Saek and other
scholars. It was supplemented and published as an appendix
of annual of Sejong. Then several years later, with the
addition of some literary works, it was completed as *Tongguk Yoji Sŏngnam* (Survey of Korean Geography) and after
several revisions, it finally was perfected to the 55-volume
Sinjung Tongguk Yoji Sŏngnam (Revised Survey of Korean
Geography) which is still kept today.

The geographical division of Korea into eight *"do"* (provinces) is clearly stated in this gazetteers as the form preceding the thirteen-*do* composition which was in use untill
recently.

The fourth accomplishment was the completion of the
statute. The work was begun in the reign of T'aejong with
the compilation of *Kyongje Yukchŏn*, which was completed
in his era. As new laws and ordinance were issued, the code
was revised, and expanded through the reigns of T'aejong,
Sejong and Sejo until it was finally completed in the first
year of Yejong (1469 A.D.) and published in the following
year as *Kyŏngguk Taejŏn* in six volumes. This laid the foundation of the administrative structure and statute for the
nation. Composed of six parts, respectively devoted to mat-
ters of civil appointment, revenue, rites, war, punishments
and works, the statute was patterned after the Chinese six-
code system with necessary modifications and the inclusion
of Korean traditions and customs to meet the local need.
Thus this statute was respected for many generations as a
great legacy of the founders of the country, and served as
the standard for administration. Any revision had to go
through a series of very strict procedures.

In close relation to the active turnout of these important

Painting of King Sejo

Nunmin Chŏngŭm,
the Oldest Hangul Manual

T'aepaek-san Library

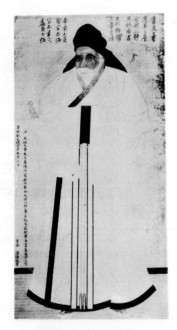

Portrait of Song Si-yŏl

Painting of a Tiger

works was the development of printing techniques. Use of printing types first became popular in the late Koryŏ period, and during the reigns of T'aejong and Sejong, hundreds of thousands of types were said to have been cast, laying the foundation for the famous Korean types.

When the cultural development of the period is viewed as a whole, one can name quite a number of great works in the fields of literature, art and craft. The most important among them was the creation of the Korean national letters known as *Hangul*.

Hangul, the use of which was promulgated in 1446 A.D., was a system of phonetic symbols like the Roman alphabet. Originally, it was composed of 28 vowels and consonants but later was rearranged into 11 vowels and 14 consonant symbols, which in combination designated all Korean sounds.

Since the Silla period, attempts had been made to employ Chinese characters to express the Korean sounds, but their use had not widely spread. The creation of the Korean phonetic symbols was thus the most epochal event in the cultural history of Korea, for it gave the common people their own symbols to put the spoken words on paper, and enabled a swift, wide spreading of culture.

As for the origin of *Hangul*, there is no agreement among scholars. One school thinks that it was a simplification of ancient Chinese seal characters. Some say it derived from old Indian script, others trace it to hieroglyphs, still others maintain that it came from the Tibetan alphabet. However, consideration of the cultural circumstances of that time suggests us the likeliest supposition that *Hangul* symbols came from Mongolian letters. Even if no direct ties are found between the two, it is easy to imagine that efforts to create the Korean symbols were motivated through frequent contacts with the Mongolian culture since the Koryŏ days.

Thus the cultural foundations for the Yi Dynasty were laid. Let us see in the next chapter how the life of the general public was regulated and what served as moral standards.

19

BUDDHISM AND CONFUCIANISM

As mentioned earlier, Buddhism received special protection under the Koryŏ rulers because of the role it played in the defense of the nation. Temples were given the protection and support of the state and priests became aristocratic after the mid-Silla period. Buddhist priests not only won the respect of all the people but also gained an increased economic power. In fact, the temples owned land and serfs, giving the priests the same economic status as aristocrats of the day.

Given such privileges and economic and political power, Buddhist priests gradually became corrupt, inviting strong criticism against Buddhism. It was only natural that once their religious sanctity was gone, the temples attracted the special attention of the administrator for their secular power.

As the Yi Dynasty was formed, aristocrats and high officials of the old regime were deprived of their lands and serfs which were taken over by those who rose to power under the new dynasty. The Buddhist temples were no exception.

T'aejo limited the number of Buddhist priests by establishing a license system under which anybody who wanted to obtain the license was first required to pay a certain tax. He inhibited construction of new temples and deprived those priests who failed to meet the qualification as a Buddhist priest of all privileges. Then in 1406 A.D. T'aejong limited the number of Buddhist sects to 12, and the total number of temples to 232, set the standard number of serfs and area of manorial land for each class of temples and confiscated all that exceeded the level.

This strict policy on Buddhism was further intensified by Sejong, who in 1424 A.D. merged various sects of Buddhism into only two, *Sŏnjong* (Practice Sect) and *Kyojong* (Learning Sect), reduced the number of head-temples to 36 and cut the number of peasants and area of land accordingly.

Thus Buddhism and Buddhist priests were suppressed in the early days of the Yi Dynasty. But no matter how depraved priests became and how harsh the persecution was, the Buddhist faith kept by individual followers did not die out. On the contrary, people looked for moral and spiritual support more earnestly at the time of a great change involving falling and rising dynasties than in times of peace. This was also true of the rulers; even of T'aejo himself, who started the anti-Buddhism policy, and also of Sejong and Sejo.

However, since the basic policy of the dynasty was to hold down Buddhism, this religion played a far inferior historical role in the day of Yi Dynasty compared with its role in the preceding Koryŏ period. The religion, or it may be better called philosophy, that was characteristic of Yi Dynasty days was Confucianism.

Although Confucianism had been known in Korea since the days of the Three Kingdoms, it was Chu-tzu's Neo-Confucianism which had a wide influence in the Yi Dynasty period. Developed in south China, Chu-tzu's philosophy spread to north China in the Yüan period, and was brought to Koryŏ by high officials and scholars who visited the Yüan capital (Peking) frequently, as Koryŏ being a subject state of the Mongols. The fact that the Yüan civil service examination was open to Koryŏ subjects added impetus to the spreading of Chu-tzu's Neo-Confucianism in Koryŏ, as it was

why were Chinese exams open at some times + closed at others?

(interesting thesis would be a study of foreigners (Koreans) who took the Chinese exams)

an important part of learning in Yüan then. Copying the Chinese system, Koryŏ soon adopted the civil service examination system, paving the road for the widespread dissemination of Chu-tzu's philosophy in Korea.

Chu-tzu's Neo-Confucianism was essentially anti-Buddhism. As corrupt Buddhist priests were drawing strong criticism and anti-Buddhistic feeling was prevailing, Korea in the early Yi Dynasty, had an ideal climate for accepting Chu-tzu's philosophy. Furthermore, the administrators made strong efforts to spread the Neo-Confucianism in line with their Buddhism reform policy by making it the state religion, by making it a compulsory item in the civil and military examinations, and by building schools to teach the religion. This was apparently done more for renewing and organizing public sentiment in support of the new regime than for merely oppressing Buddhism.

Chu-tzu's Neo-Confucianism also served as the standard for the new social order, regulations, and manners. In the Koryŏ days, both official and private functions and rites were performed in the Buddhist manner; now Neo-Confucianism replaced it. The most fundamental and concrete standards of the manners of Chu-tzu's Neo-Confucianism were laid in *Wen-Kung Chia-li*, said to be authored by Chu-tzu himself. This book set the regulations for the ceremonies of coming of age, marriage, and funerals for the ruling class. Centering on ancestral worship, it strictly differentiated the position of each family member and related social distinctions, sharply contrasting the philosophy of Buddhism which called for absolute equality.

These basic principles and practical regulations originally set for the rulers were adopted by the common people, and became an integral part of their life, their traces still being observed in the customs and manners of Koreans today.

However, the manners set forth by Chu-tzu's philosophy tended to be superficial and the fundamentals of Neo-Confucianism placed excessive emphasis on knowledge and moral obligations, thus binding the life and customs of the people with mannerism. Furthermore, when it came to giving spiritual comfort or saving one's soul, this new philosophy was not comparable to Buddhism. This weakness of Neo-Confucianism accounts for the continued influence Buddhism commanded over the people in spite of all the oppressive measures it experienced under the Yi regime. That Shamanism became quite popular among the common people was also attributable to the shortcomings of Chu-tzu's philosophy.

In short, Chu-tzu's Neo-Confucianism had outstanding merit in bringing about unity among the people but it also did harm when the unity turned into uniformity, then to stagnancy and to degeneration. It became involved in power struggles in the court and then in disputes between political parties which were to fill the pages of the history of the later Yi Dynasty period.

20

PARTY STRIFE

A series of conflicts between political parties was heralded by the internal struggle between the royal court officials during the reign of King Yŏnsan. Since the trouble had direct bearing on the succession to the throne, let me briefly touch on the succession to the throne after T'aejo.

A year after his accession to the throne, T'aejo named Pangsŏk, born by his second queen Kang, as Crown Prince. Since the young Crown Prince had many brothers by different mothers, a senior minister Chŏng Tojŏn attempted to kill these princes in fear of a possible struggle over the throne between the Crown Prince and his brothers. However, this plot leaked out, and one of the princes, Pangwŏn, assassinated the Crown Prince and Chŏng, and asked his father to name his elder brother Panggwa the new Crown Prince. T'aejo accepted this request, and abdicated from the throne to Panggwa (later Chŏngjong). T'aejo named himself ex-King and held the title for ten years after that.

Chŏngjong, on the other hand, vacated his throne to his young brother Pangwŏn (later T'aejong) in only two years. The throne was passed from T'aejong to his son Sejong, then to Munjong, who perished in two years. The then Crown Prince (later Tanjong) took the throne at the age of twelve. It was 60 odd years after its founding that the Yi Dynasty faced a serious crisis with the enthronement of this young King Tanjong.

Tangjong's uncle Prince Suyang (Sejo) killed key retainers who had assisted Tanjong on the orders of King Munjong, and claimed the throne himself. Then he further killed more than 70 high government officials, who attempted to restore the throne to King Tanjong, and finally killed Tanjong (Nosangun) himself.

Sejo's son Yejong died a year after this enthronement, and was succeeded by his son Sŏngjong, whose reign lasted for 25 years in fairly good repute. However, his successor Yŏnsan was dissolute in conduct and known for many failures in his policies. A military official Han Myŏnghoe and his family who helped Sejo to take the throne established a maternal relationship with the king's family and grasped the actual power of the government. On the other hand, theorist statemen in the group of Kim Chongjik who had held important posts during the reign of King Sŏngjong were opposed to the Han Myŏnghoe's group. The conflicts between these two groups came to the fore over the historical interpretation of Sejo's enthronement in 1498 A.D.

Kim Chongjik's school is believed to have originated by

Kil Chae, a Confucianist who served to Kings U and Ch'ang during the late days of Koryŏ. After those two kings were killed by their political enemies, Kil Chae retired from official service and dedicated his life to the education of youth at his home town, Sŏnsan, Kyŏngsang-do.

One of his students, Kim Sukcha, a son of a local official, was invited to serve the government by King Sejong and made his name as a government scholar. Kim Chongjik was one of his sons.

Kim Chongjik's students included Kim Ilson, Kim Hongp'il, Chŏng Yŏch'ang and many other notables who together formed an influential academic group. This group, called a theorist group against the conventional rhetorician group, emphasized the moral criticism of the Chu-tzu school.

In 1498 A.D., Kim Chongjik's disciple, Kim Ilson was criticized by his opponent group for having written criticism against Sejo in his historical study. Members of his group were either killed or ousted from the central Government to remote areas. Six years later, the remaining members of his group were all executed.

King Chungjong who replaced Yŏnsan first made important Cho Kwangjo who inherited Kim Chongjik's theory, but gradually became dissatisfied with their policy. Then, the opposition group took this opportunity to drive Cho Kwangjo and his group out of power, in 1519 A.D. Thus, the Chu-tzu school group was forced to retreat. However, this did not put an end to the fights among high government officials at all. When Chungjong's successor Injong perished only eight months after his enthronement, and his brother Myŏngjong took the throne at the age of twelve, the power struggle between Yun Im and Yun Wŏnhyŏng, the two relatives of the King's family, grew keener. The Chu-tzu group was also involved in this struggle. Because the group was regarded as siding with the Yun Im's camp, it was oppressed severely by Yun Wŏnhyŏng's group. Among the members of the Chu-tzu group at that time were Yi Hwang (T'oegye) and Yi I (Yulgok), who are deemed to have been Korea's top-notch Confucianists.

Myŏngjong's successor Sŏnjo promoted members of the Chu-tzu group to high government posts at first. However, the idealism of these new thinkers did not go well with the conservative attitude of government leaders at that time. Thus, the tension between the old and the new grew keener. In addition, the intraparty struggle between members of the Chu-tzu group developed from this time on in an increasing seriousness.

Meanwhile, Chief Justice Sin Ŭigyŏn, brother to the Queen of King Myŏngjong, and Kim Hyowŏn, a relative of Yun Wŏnhyŏng and a disciple of the Kim Chongjik school, were pitted against each other in fierce rivalry over a power struggle. The two were surrounded by hundreds of followers —the former for his high family status and high government post, and the latter for his academic fame, intelligence, and the post of appointing government officials. Sin Ŭigyŏn's group was called *Sŏin* (Westerners) while Kim Hyowŏn's group was called *Tongin* (Easterners). Later, the *Tongin* group was split into two groups—*Namin* (Southerners) and *Pugin* (Northerners). The three groups are known together as the 'three colors' (See the list in page 73).

The history of the Yi Dynasty is said to be the history of party struggles. These three groups observed repeated splits among themselves, but maintained their schools for 300 years, each developing strong, executive characteristics. While the king's power was too weak to settle those party struggles, each group engaged in an endless struggle one against another. It was only natural that their conduct had unfavorable influence over national policy and the social life of the public.

21

JAPANESE INVASION OF KOREA

While Korean politics were thrown into confusion because of repeated party struggles since the time of King Yŏnsan, Japanese troops crossed the sea to approach the waters off Pusan. This incident in 1592 A.D. gave a tremendous shock to both the government and the people of Korea.

Toyotomi Hideyoshi, a Japanese warlord who was about to put the whole of Japan under his control at that time, attempted to expand into Continental Asia. In 1589 A.D., he ordered Sō Yoshitomo, the lord of Tsushima Island, to ask the Korean king to swear his allegiance to Japan. As far as the Sō family was concerned, however, the relationship between Japan and Korea had important implications for commercial trade between Tsushima Island and Korea. Therefore, Sō himself visited Korea to have negotiations with Korean leaders, and narrowly persuaded them to send a two-man mission to Japan, and brought it to Japan. Hideyoshi told the mission that he had a definite plan to attack Ming, China, and asked them to tell the Korean king to serve in the vanguard of the Japanese expeditionary forces to Ming.

However, the Korean king failed to give an explicit answer to Hideyoshi's request, in spite of desperate efforts by Sō. Thus, Hideyoshi turned his target from Ming to Korea. He sent an army of 160,000 men across the sea to the peninsula.

The Japanese army landed at Pusan in April, 1592 A.D., and in only 20 days, took Seoul by a lightening attack. The Korean king Sŏnjo having failed to take immediate defensive measure against the Japanese invasion, abandoned the capital to flee to the north, and entered P'yŏngyang. During the exodus from Seoul to P'yŏngyang, the King sent Prince Sunhwa to Kangwŏn-do and Prince Imhae to Hamgyŏng-do to raise troops there.

After entering Seoul, Japanese commanders got together to decide which troop should attack which area, and continued the aggression in Korea, collecting taxes from residents to secure foodstuffs for the Japanese soldiers.

The Japanese troops that entered P'yŏngan-do occupied P'yŏngyang to force the Korean King to abandon the city and to go up farther north to Ŭiju. Meanwhile, the troops that headed for Hamgyŏng-do captured Princes Sunhwa and Imhae in Hoenyŏng, then crossed the Tumen River to enter the land of Orangk'ae or Warka, a Tungusic people living in East Manchuria. Other areas were also taken by the Japanese troops. The Korean navy, headed by Yi Sunsin, alone maintained its superiority over the Japanese navy throughout the war.

In the meantime, Ming determined to help her subordinate country fight back the Japanese invasion, and Ming General Tsu Ch'eng-hsün headed an army to attack P'yŏngyang by way of Liao-tung in June, but without success. Then, Ming sent Shen Wei-ching as a peace envoy to the Japanese camp in an effort to check the sharp advance of the Japanese troops and to investigate the situation of the Japanese troops in Korea. He met Japanese commanders in P'yŏngyang for the negotiations, and after returning home, advised the Government to conclude a peace treaty with Japan. However, the Ming Government ignored his advice and sent the army of General Li Ju-sung to attack P'yŏngyang next January, 1593 A.D. The Japanese troops retreated from P'yŏngyang, and narrowly checked the advance of the Ming troops in the northwestern suburbs of Seoul.

Meanwhile, the "rescue army" of Ming encouraged the Korean people to organize militias here and there in the

peninsula. The Japanese troops had great trouble in sub-
duing these Korean resistance fronts. It was in such circumstances that Shen Wei-ching visited Konishi Yukinaga,
one of the Japanese commanders, in Seoul to seek for an
armistice treaty. The proposed terms were exchange of peace
missions between the two countries and simultaneous withdrawal of the troops from the peninsula.

The negotiations, however, failed in 1596 A.D. as a wide
gap became apparent between the Ming court and Hideyoshi
in the appraisal of the situation. Early the next year, the
Japanese troops landed in southern Korea. Ming also mobilized her army and navy on the request of Korea to counter-
attack the Japanese troops. Thus, Japanese and Ming troops
engaged in fierce battles again.

Before the Japanese army registered any sizable victory,
Hideyoshi succumbed to an illness, ordering in his will
withdrawal of Japanese troops. Konishi Yukinaga, who was
dealing with the peace negotiations with Ming representa-
tives since the previous war, conferred with Ming commanders and exchanged hostages. After the two parties agreed
that Korea would sent an armistice mission later to Japan,
Konishi withdrew the Japanese troops from Korea. Thus,
the seven-year long war came to a tentative end.

It was a great setback to Korea that it engaged in the
long, repeated war against Japan, especially in the southern
half of the peninsula which was rich in agricultural resources, and that the Ming troops stayed in Korea for a
long time after Japan's withdrawal, squeezing Korea's
wealth. The overall interpretation of the historical meaning
of this war should be reviewed through a study of the war's
influence over Korea's political, social and economical structure.

The repeated dispatch of large armies to Korea was a
fatal blow to the already-weakening power of Ming and
constituted a major factor towards Ming's fall through the

financial difficulties of the country. On the other hand, the decadence of Ming resulted in the rise of the up-and-coming Manchu power—Nurhachi, headman of the Jurchin tribe based in the area around Yenden, east of Mukden.

In spite of the armistice treaty concluded between Japan's Konishi and the Ming commanders, Korea did not send its mission to Japan after all. It was in the 17th century when the Tokugawa Shogunate was established that Korea's attitude to Japan became more favorable. Tsushima's lord Sō Yoshitomo made his own efforts to restore Japan-Korea diplomatic relations with the hope of restoring trade relations between Tsushima and Korea for his own economic reasons.

As a result, a Korean peace mission visited Japan in 1607 A.D. and diplomatic relations between the two countries were officially restored. After that, Korea sent 12 missions to Japan throughout the 300 years of the Tokugawa era. In 1609 A.D., Sō Yoshitomo himself concluded a trade treaty with Korea. The treaty, thus monopolized by Tsushima on the Japanese side, was aimed principally at receiving from Korea supplies of goods which were short in Tsushima, with a view to stabilizing people's life in the Island. Therefore, trade on a mutual exchange basis was given secondary importance under the treaty. Under this treaty, Sō purchased 100 *sŏk* of rice from Korea, and in return sent 20 trade ships to Korea every year. Pusan was designated as the sole Korean port open to Tsushima for the purpose of trade, and a Japanese consulate was opened there for the reception of the trade ships. Sō had his officials stay in the consulate in Pusan to deal with the Tsushima-Korea trade business.

This consulate house was located on the Chŏryŏng Island off Pusan Port during the years immediately following the withdrawal of the Japanese army, but moved to Such'ang-dong (then Tumop'u), south of Pusan City after the treaty was concluded. The consulate house was moved to Ch'oryang 70 years later and remained there for 200 years until the late 19th century.

Japan exported domestic-made copper as well as such imported items as dyestuffs, buffalow horn and pepper, and imported from Korea rice, soy beans, cotton, carrots and herb medicines.

22

KOREA'S RELATIONSHIP WITH MING AND CH'ING

Even the seven-year-long war failed to dissolve the aforementioned party struggles in Korea. Each party was unable to get rid of its exclusively closed characteristics in spite of the life and death crisis in the country. The rivalling political principles remained separate throughout the war.

King Sŏngjo's successor Kwanghae was dethroned by the *Sŏin* group, which helped Injo to the throne. Thus, the accession to the throne became to be a tool of the party struggles.

A few years after the enthronement of King Injo, Korea faced its second threat from the northern enemy—invasion by the Ch'ing Army in 1627 A.D.

Nurhachi, the first Emperor of Ch'ing, raised his army in Yenden, Manchuria, in early 1580's and expanded his power while Korea was engaged in the war against Japan. He conquered Jurchin tribes who lived in northern Manchuria, and named his country Latter Chin in 1616 A.D. After scoring an overwhelming victory in the battle with the Ming army at Mt. Sarhū, he took Shen-yang (Mukden) and Liao-yang, then placed the whole of the Liao-tung area under his control before he moved the capital to Shen-yang.

At the battle of Mt. Sarhū, Korea sent her army in response to Ming's request, and attacked Manchu troops from the south. As the Ming army was defeated in the battle, however, Korean Commander-in-Chief Kang Hongnip and Vice-Commander Kim Kyŏngsŏ surrendered themselves to Manchu troops.

Nurhachi's successor Hong Taiji sent an army of 30,000 men to Korea, which had refused to surrender to him for its allegiance to Ming. When the Korean King Injo received the report that the Manchu Army reached P'yŏngsan, Hwanghae-do, he took refuge on Kanghwa Island, and sent an armistice mission to the invaders. Thus, Korea concluded an alliance with the Manchus, and swore to send a tributary mission to the Manchu court regularly. The Manchu army returned to the north. (1627 A.D.)

Nine years later, Latter Chin changed its name to Ch'ing. As Korea later showed signs of restoring its subordinate relationship to Ming, Ch'ing's Hong Taiji himself led a large army to attack Korea. As Manchu troops approached Seoul, the Korean King tried to escape to Kanghwa Island again, but had no time to do so, and entered the Namhansan Castle in Kangju with his Crown Prince. The castle was soon besieged by the Ch'ing army, and Injo surrendered to Ch'ing only 45 days later. He was forced to pledge Korea's absolute subordination to Ch'ing by cutting Korea's relationship with Ming, to submit hostages and to deploy Korean troops when requested by Ch'ing. As he accepted more than ten severe conditions for Korea's allegiance to Ch'ing, Hong Taiji approved Korea's surrender in the Namhansan Castle. There is a monument with the inscriptions written in Manchu, Mongolian and Chinese to mark the surrender at Samch'ŏndo on the bank of the Han River, where the Manchu Emperor accepted Injo's surrender.

Thus having conquered Korea to secure the safety of its own flank, Ch'ing started the invasion of northern China seven years later, and moved its capital to Peking in 1644 A.D.

After the surrender to Ch'ing at Namhansan Castle, Korea sent four official missions to the Ch'ing capital every year. Besides these four official, annual missions, (which were later made into one mission a year) Korea sent additional "extraordinary" missions with a quantity of contributions to the Emperor.

The annual contribution included 100 taels of gold, 1,000 taels of silver, 200 pairs of buffalow-horn bowends, 100 sheets of leopard skin, 100 sheets of deer skin, 1,000 packs of tea, 400 sheets of otter skin, 300 sheets of leather, 10 packs of pepper, 26 swords, 200 catties of Sapan-wood, 1,000 rolls of large-sized papers, 10 short swords, 1,500 rolls of small-sized papers, 4 grass sheets with five-nailed dragon patterns, 40 grass sheets with flowers patterns, 200 rolls of ramie cloth, 2,000 rolls of mixed cotton-silk cloth, 400 rolls of hemp cloth, 10,000 rolls of fine cotton cloth, 1,400 rolls of ordinary cotton cloth, and 1,000 sacks of rice.

The forced tribute to Ch'ing by Korea lasted until toward the end of the Yi Dynasty, though its quantity was gradually reduced. On the other hand, anti-Ch'ing feeling among the Korean people enhanced their respect to the defunct Ming culture, which constituted the main stream of thought during the latter half of the Yi Dynasty.

23

NEW TREND IN LEARNING

Although Korea changed its subordination to Ch'ing from Ming, the domestic party struggles continued. In fact, the party struggles grew worse year after year and decade after decade. With the worsening of the party struggles, thousand of able government officials were killed by their enemies, and the king's reign grew weaker every age. The history of these party struggles from King Sŏnjo's time can be roughly illustrated as in the following list (See page 73).

Thus, about 100 years after the formation of the Easterners (*Tongin*) and the Westerners, the Korean scholars and officialdom were divided roughly into four groups—*Noron* (Old Doctoriners), *Soron* (Young Doctoriners), *Namin* (Southerners) and *Pugin* (Northerners)—under the reign of King Sukchong.

From the Sukchong Age on, the scholars and thinkers in the central government posts belonged either to the *Noron* or *Soron* groups which engaged in fierce rivalry. The *Namin* group lost its former glory and fame and faded away from that time.

Song Siryŏl, one of the famed leaders of the *Noron* group, was a noted scholar of the time, but was executed in 1689 A.D., victim of the opposition's intrigues.

King Kyŏngjong, whose reign succeeded the 46-year-long reign of King Sukchong, perished four years later, and was succeeded by Yŏngjo who was on the throne for 52 years. Then, Chŏngjo replaced Yŏngjo and ruled the country for 24 years.

Korean culture flourished during the 76 years of the rules of Kings Yŏngjo and Chŏngjo, in what is called the second

	1567 A.D.	1608	1623	1649	1674	1720
Reigns	Sŏnjo	Kwanghae-gun	Injo	Hyŏjong & Hyŏnjong	Sukchong	
Factions						

Tongin (Easterners) —
- Namin (Southerner) ——— Namin ——— Namin ——— Namin ——— Ch'ongnam ——— Namin
  - T'angnam ——— Namin
- Pugin (Northerner) —
  - Taebuk —
    - Chungbuk
    - Yukbuk
    - Kolbuk
  - Sobuk —
    - Ch'ongsobuk
    - T'aksobuk ——— Sobuk ——— Pugin

Sŏin (Westerners) —
- Yun-sŏ
- Sin-sŏ ——— Sŏin —
  - Ch'ongsŏ
  - Kongsŏ —
    - Nosŏ
    - Sosŏ ——— Sŏin ——— Noron ——— Noron
    - Soron ——— Soron

prosperity period of the Korean culture (during the Yi Dynasty, after the one which occurred under King Sejong.) Both Yŏngjo and Chŏngjo were cultured, clever kings, who took men of talent into government services by fair selection, in an attempt to eliminate the ugly power struggles between political parties.

The cultural prosperity of the period was also attributable to the rise of the *Namin* group in scholarly fields. After its retreat from political struggles, the *Namin* group sought its *raison d'être* in scientific fields, especially in such practical sciences as history, geography and constitutional study. Also rising to leading positions in the society at that time were members of the so-called "middle class", which consisted of those who had been ranked in between the ruling upper class and the common, as well as those of underprivileged status, such as children of mistresses who had been given discriminatory treatment even though their fathers were of the upper class. Those "new class" people were given the opportunity to serve in high government posts provided they passed examinations for such practical sciences as translation, jurisprudence, mathematics and medical sciences.

Thus, the cultural prosperity of Korea at that time was affected by external influences, particularly from China. The 70 odd years under the reign of the Kings Yŏngjo and Chŏngjo in Korea corresponded roughly with the Ch'ien-lung Era (60 years) when the cultural development of the Ch'ing Dynasty reached its peak. During the late days of the Ming Dynasty, the Ming Government enforced strict restrictions on the activities in China of Korean missions, particularly in terms of their approach to Ming scholars. The Ming Government even restricted the purchase by Korean mission members of Chinese publications in Ming.

These restrictions were largely lifted after the Ch'ing took over the control of China. Korean mission members were permitted to visit noted Chinese scholars in Peking and to buy Chinese publications, both classic and contemporary. Thus, the methodology of historical researches in Ch'ing at that time was introduced to Korea to flourish in the peninsula during the age of King Chŏngjo.

It must be noted that Western sciences and Christianity were also introduced to Korea via China. It was at this age that Korea imported from China the Western sciences of astronomy, mathematics and artillery. Christianity seemed to have been studied by Korean scholars as a school of philosophy, rather than as a religion. An Chŏngbok, a noted scholar of the *Namin* group, wrote books on Christianity at that time.

Christianity as a philosophy gradually took on the form of a religion in Korea, attracting a growing number of believers. In 1795 A.D., a Chinese missionary Chou Wen-mu visited Korea, followed by French missionaries on a series of visit. Shocked by the rapid development of the Western religion in Korea, the Korean government, which at first paid little attention to Christianity, started placing restrictions on the activities of Christian missionaries in Korea (1801 A.D.). Then, the government bolstered restrictions on Christianity in 1839 and 1866 A.D.

New trends in Korean sciences were symbolically expressed by the establishment of an organ called Kyujanggak, which was set up at the Royal Court in the early years of King Chŏngjo. This organ can be termed an entirely new kind of Korean academic center, free from the conventional administrative controls and from the control of relatives of the royal family and government officials who had held a tremendous power over Korean scholars. Legally speaking, however, this organ was meant for preserving the writings of Korean kings and for collecting and storing Korean and Chinese classical books. The collection of classic publications appeared to follow the example of the Chinese *Ssu-k'u Ch'üan-shu* of the Ch'ien-lung Age. The leading management posts of the Kyujanggak were held by *Kŏmsŏgwan* or Book Inspectors. Pak Chega, Sŏ Isu, Yi Tŭngmu and Yu Tukkong who were appointed as first managers of the organ were all of the aforementioned "New class", while some others, including Chŏng Yagyong and Yi Kahwan, were scholars of the *Namin* group and personal assistants to King Chŏngjo.

The writings of the Chŏngjo who was also known under the pen name of Hongjae, were arranged into the 100 volumes of *Hongjae Ch'ŏnsŏ*. This collection describes the life of Chŏngjo as an individual on the one hand and his policy on Korean culture on the other hand, thereby showing the cultural taste of statesmen as well as men of culture as that time in Korea.

The period of about 50 years after the death of Chŏngjo, which was under the reigns of Sunjo and Hyŏngjong, was regarded as a politically decadence period in Korea. In terms of cultural development, however, the period witnessed a maturity of the Korean culture which was planted during the Chŏngjo Age. One of the representative scholars at that time was Kim Chŏnghŭi, who was said to be a rare genius. He gained friendship with such great Chinese scholars of the Ch'ien-lung Age as Weng Fang-kang and Yüan Yüan, and was credited with propagating the practical approach he learned from Chinese scholars throughout the peninsula.

24

FOREIGN POWERS AND KOREA

Around the turn of the eighteenth century, Asian countries began to feel increasing pressure from European and American powers. This was touched off by the Opium War which resulted in the five open ports of China, Canton, Foochow, Ningpo, Amoy and Shanghai, for foreign trade in 1842 under the Nanking Treaty. It is frequently said that one of the aftermaths of this was Japan's opening of its doors to foreigners only twelve years later, lifting the 300-year old ban on foreign trade. It was only natural that Korea could not be left out of the resulting Western Influence.

At that time Korea saw a succession of infant monarchs, headed by King Sunjo who came to the throne at the age of eleven, resulting in increased intervention in politics by the royal in-laws, though it had been previously suppressed under King Chŏngjo. After the death of King Ch'ŏljong in 1863 A.D., however, Yi Siüng, father of the newly enthroned king Kojong, came to power, thus changing the pattern. The title of Hŭngsŏn Taewŏngun was conferred on him, and he is commonly known simply as Taewŏngun.

Taewŏngun, a regent forceful and quick in making decisions, gathered around him many talented persons, demonstrated his power by rebuilding the Kyŏngbok Palace, and tried to break social stagnancy by reforming traditional institutions. In his persecution of Christianity, some French missionaries were killed. This provoked the French authority residing in China to send warships, which sailed up to the Korean coast and bombarded Kanghwa Island in 1866 A.D. In the same year, the American fleet came to Korea demanding an explanation about an incident in which the Sherman, an American tradeship, was burned and plundered on the Taedong River in the previous year. Both fleets had to withdraw before the strong defense of the Koreans, and Taewŏngun's anti-alien attitude was even more strengthened.

Meanwhile in Japan a rapid reform was in progress, the so-called Meiji Restoration in 1868 A.D. The new Japanese regime at once started an attempt to establish diplomatic relations with Korea, but encountered Korea's stubborn refusal. In 1873 A.D. the Korean king reached maturity and Taewŏngun retired as the regent and left the seat of power. Now the center of politics shifted to the house of Min, from which Kojong's queen came. Long hostile to Taewŏngun, the Mins reversed Taewŏngun's policies to the last item, and Korea's attitude toward foreigners relaxed somewhat so that an informal negotiation was opened for diplomatic relations between her and Japan.

In August of 1875A.D., the Japanese warship Un'yŏ was bombarded while sailing off Kanghwa from a Korean fortress on the Island. The ship at once withdrew, then attacked and occupied another Korean fortress. Because of this incident, Japan dispatched a delegation headed by the Japanese high officials Kuroda Kiyotaka and Inoue Kaoru to Korea in February of the next year, and the eleven articles on the Treaty of Amity were concluded at Kanghwa, followed by the eleven supplementary articles of the Treaty and the eleven-article Commercial Treaty signed in Seoul in August of the same year. Under these treaties, the port of Pusan was opened for trade first, then Wŏnsan in 1879 A.D. and Inchŏn in 1883 A.D. It was this Korean-Japanese treaty of 1876 that enabled Western powers to open formal relations with Korea in subsequent years.

Thus Korea after the resignation of Taewŏngun was taking steps toward modernization. Taewŏngun and his clique were not very pleased at this. In 1862 A.D., joined by those antagonistic to the Mins, they incited the Korean soldiers to attack the royal palace. The Queen Min and her kinsmen were wiped out. The Japanese legation was also attacked. Requested by the Korean ambassador, the Chinese sent troops to Korea, arrested Taewŏngun and took his away to put him in custody in Tientsin, and their troops remained stationed in Seoul. The Chemulp'o Treaty was newly concluded between Korea and Japan, under which Japan received an apology and reparations and was permitted, too, to station troops in Seoul.

This was the time when antagonism between the progressives and the conservatives was growing stronger in Korea. The progressives were headed by young politicians Hong Yŏngjik and Kim Okkyun, while the conservatives consisted of the royal inlaws, Min and Cho Houses, and their adherents. The progressives attempted a coup d'état in 1884 A.D. aimed at toppling the regime of their opponents and seizing power under the Japanese assistance, causing the Chinese and the Japanese troops to engage in a battle. This problem was settled in the next year by the Seoul Treaty between Korea and Japan and the Tientsin Treaty between China and Japan, after which both countries withdrew their troops from the Korean Peninsula. Yet another Sino-Japanese conflict was to come because of the Tonghak Rebellion.

The Tonghak Party had its origin in the Tonghak-do, a religion founded by Ch'oe Cheu, a native of Kyŏngju, Kyŏngsang-pukto, mixing doctrines of Confucianism, Buddhism and Taoism. Though his teaching was strongly opposed to Christianity, then banned and held evil in Korea, his followers were more interested in politics, sometimes plotting a revolt, and thereby arousing the suspicions of officialdom. As soon as Chŏn Pongjun arose in arms at Chŏngŭp, Chŏlla-pukto, to protest against the local authority's injustice in 1894 A.D., his fellow Tonghak believers responded to him by widespread uprisings in Chŏlla-namdo, Chŏlla-pukto, Ch'ungch'ŏng-namdo, and Ch'ungch'ŏng-pukto. This rebellion proved too big to

be suppressed by the Mins then in power, who asked China
for military assistance. The Chinese sent troops in, at the
same time giving Japan notice according to the Tientsin
Treaty. Japan too sent troops and joined the Chinese in putting down the rebellion.

Since the Tonghak Rebellion was a result of the corruption of the Korean government, Japan intended to take this
chance to introduce a new political system to Korea in order
to prevent further international strife. China would not give
consent to the Japanese proposal, and the Sino-Japanese War
broke out.

The victory of the Japanese liberated Korea from the
Chinese domination, and even before peace was restored by
the Shimonoseki Treaty in the April of 1895 A.D., the Korean political system was thoroughly modernized in the
so-called Reform of 1894 A.D. The next year a new era,
Kŏnyang, was adopted, and in 1895 A.D. the name of the
kingdom was changed from Chosŏn to the Great Han Empire. Not everybody was happy with the Reform, however.
The Mins rose again taking advantage of this situation,
seized power and adopted reactionary politics. It was Russia
who exerted much influence in Korea of that time.

When China was defeated by Japan and revealed her
weakness before the world, Russia, Germany and France
claimed that Japan's occupation of the Liao-tung Peninsula
was harmful to the peace of the Far East and advised Japan
to return it to China. Japan could not nothing but follow the
advice. Then the three powers exploited the intervention as
pretext of extracting concessions from China. Among them,
the most important was that Russia in 1898 took Lü-shun
(Port Arthur) and Dairen (Dalnyi) under the guise of a
25-year lease and was given the right to build railways to
connect them with the Siberian Railways. As this had a
great bearing on the security of Korea, Japan made an
entente with Russia and the countries promised mutually

Gate of Kanghwa, Seoul

Hŭngsŏn Taewŏngun

Kojong,
Emperor of Han Empire

Russian Legation in Seoul

not to interfere with the internal politics of Korea.

In 1900, taking advantage of the breakout of an anti-alien movement—the Boxer Rebellion—in China, Russia sent a big army into Manchuria and would not withdraw even after the rebellion was over. This was nothing less than an actual annexation of Manchuria, and caused much alarm to both China and Korea. As the Russian army moved into the Korean Peninsula, Japan tried to negotiate with the Russians for the sake of Korea's protection. Russia would not give up her desire to dominate Korea and put strong pressure upon Japanese activity in Korea. Under such circumstances, Japan declared war upon Russia in February, 1904 A.D.

25

JAPANESE RULE AND LIBERATION

With the outbreak of the Russo-Japanese war, Japan concluded a defense alliance with Korea, making Russia a common enemy of the two countries. In addition, Japan concluded diplomatic and financial agreements with Korea to tighten the relations between the two nations.

In the Treaty of Peace signed at Portsmouth on September 5, 1905, the Imperial Russian Government pledged that "acknowledging that Japan possesses in Korea paramount political, military and economical interests, (the Russian Government) will engage neither to obstruct nor interfere with the measures of guidance, protection and control which the Imperial Government of Japan may find it necessary to take in Korea."

Thereon, Japan concluded in November that year the Protective Agreement with Korea, took over the diplomatic rights and made Korea a protectorate of Japan. For govern-

ing the protectorate, Japan established the office of Residency-General in Seoul and made Ito Hirobumi the first
Resident-General.

The growing resistance of Koreans against the Japanese
rule first took shape in the form of dispatching of a secret
mission to the International Peace Conference at the Hague
held in June, 1907. Taking the blame for the incident, the
Korean Emperor Kojong abdicated.

Under the new Emperor Sunjong, Resident-General Ito
signed new agreements with the Korean Government for
strengthening the Japanese control over the domestic affairs
of Korea. The resistances by the Koreans against this tight-
ened grip of the Japanese culminated in the assassination of
Ito in October, 1909 and the unsuccessful attempt at the life
of Korean Prime Minister Yi Wanyong in December the
same year.

These incidents promoted Japan to decide on the annexation of Korea by force. Terauchi Masatake who was appointed the third Resident-General of Korea while holding
the office of War Minister, concluded after a series of negotiations with Prime Minister Yi the treaty for annexation
of Korea on August 22, 1910.

On September 30 that year, the new system of Government-
General of Chōsen was promulgated and on October 1, the
new ruling system went into effect.

After the annexation, Japan made every effort not to
refer to Korea as a colony, but in fact, Korea was nothing
but a Japanese colony. While emphasizing the assimilation
of Koreans with Japanese and pledging to give the same
treatment to Korea as done in Japan proper, the Japanese
rulers laid a powerful network of military police to maintain
order, and made extensive efforts to develop Korea into an
important market for the growth of the Japanese capital-
ism. Toward the end of the Japanese rule as the military
campaigns of Japan grew from the Manchurian Incident to

Sino-Japanese War and finally to the Pacific War, Korea increased its economic and military values for Japan.

All these years, the anti-Japanese resistance movements among the Koreans never ceased. Worthy of special mention is the nationwide revolt known as "Mansei Charge Incident" or "Samil Movement" which took place on March 1, 1919 on the day the funeral services of the former Korean Emperor Kojong were held. This incident is generally recognized as having marked the start of the independence movement of Korea. As a result of this incident, the grip of the Japanese military police was relaxed a little but the independence movement in Korea went underground, leaving active campaigns in the hands of Koreans outside Korea.

Toward the end of World War II, the leaders of the United States, Great Britain and China declared in the Cairo Declaration: "The aforesaid three Great Powers, mindful of the enslavement of the people of Korea, are determined that in due course Korea shall become free and independent." This position was reaffirmed in the Potsdam Proclamation of July 26, 1945 which was signed, in addition to the three powers of the Cairo Declaration, by the Soviet Union immediately after she declared war on Japan.

On August 15, 1945, with the surrender of Japan to the Allied Powers, U.S. forces moved into Korea. On September 9, Governor-General Abe Nobuyuki signed the instrument of surrender. Two days later, the U.S. Military Administration of Korea was set up in Seoul.

On the other hand, the Soviet Union sent its forces into Korea through Hamgyŏng-pukto and by the end of August, Russian forces had moved to most parts of the northern Korea. The Russians gave administrative rights mainly to the Preparation Committee for the New Korean Nation, which consisted of Communist leaders of Korea.

The areas occupied by the American and Soviet forces were divided at the 38th Parallel. At first, it was a temporary military convention. But as the time went on, the division at the 38th Parallel became *fait accompli* as the internal situation of Korea, international circumstances and foreign policies of the United States and the Soviet Union caused Korea to remain split.

On August 15, 1948, the Republic of Korea was established in South Korea and on September 8 the same year, the Democratic People's Republic of Korea came into being on the North Korean soil.

APPENDIX I

BIBLIOGRAPHY

A) REFERENCE WORKS

Korea: An Annotated Bibliography of Publications in Western Languages, Library of Congress, Washington, 1950.

Korea: An Annotated Bibliography of Publications in the Russian Language, Library of Congress, Washington, 1950.

Korea: An Annotated Bibliography of Publications in Far Eastern Languages, Library of Congress, Washington, 1950.

Marcus, Richard (ed.); *Korean Studies Guide,* University of California Press, 1954; Backus, R. L. (ed.); *Russian Supplement to the Korean Studies Guide,* 1958.

Bibliography of Korean Studies. A bibliographical guide to Korean publications on Korean studies appearing from 1945 to 1958, Asiatic Research Center, Korea University, 1961.

Asiatic Research Bulletin, Asiatic Research Center, Korea University (Ten times a year), 1958-1963, (Vol. 5, No. 10), seq.

B) PERIODICALS

Transactions of the Korean Branch of the Royal Asiatic Society, Seoul, The Society, 1900-1941; 1948-1962, (Vol. 39), irregular, seq.

Chindan Hakpo (Journal of the Chindan Society), Chindan Society, Seoul, 1934-41, 1945-50, 1955-1963, (Vol. 24), seq.

Yoksa-Hakpo (The Korean Historical Review), The Ko-

rean Historical Association, Seoul, quarterly, 1952-
1962 (No. 19), seq.

Sahak Yuenku (The Study of History), The Historical
Society of Korea, Seoul, quarterly, 1958-1963 (No. 15),
seq.

Asea Yŏn'gu (Journal of Asiatic Studies), Asiatic Research Center, Korea University, semiannual, 1957-62
(Vol. 5, No. 2), seq.

Yoksa-Kwahak (Historical Science), Academy of Sciences, P'yŏngyang, monthly, bimonthly, 1955-1963,
seq.

Yoksa Nonmunjip (Collection of Essays on Korean History), Academy of Sciences, P'yŏngyang, annual (?),
1957-61 (vol. 5).

Munhwa Yusan (Cultural Heritage), Academy of Sciences, P'yŏngyang, bimonthly, 1959 (?)-, seq.

Seikyū-gakusō (Journal of the Seikyū Society), Seikyū Gakkai, Keijō (Seoul), quarterly, 1930-1939. 30
vols.

Chōsen-gakuhō (Journal of the Academic Association of
Koreanology in Japan), Chōsen Gakkai, Tenri, quarterly, 1951-1963 (No. 28), seq.

Chōsen-kenkyūnempō (Annual Bulletin of Korean Studies), Chōsen Kenkyūkai (Association of Korean
Studies), Kyoto, 1959-1963 (No. 5), seq.

C) RESEARCH WORKS

1. Korean Publications*

a) *General Works*

Chindan Hakhoe; *Hanguksa* (History of Korea). vol. 1,

---

* For more exhaustive lists of publications in the Republic of Korea, the reader is referred to *Bibliography of
Korean Studies* and *Asiatic Research Bulletin*, mentioned-
above in column (A).

Ancient History by Yi Pyŏngdo & Kim Chaewŏn; vol. 2, Middle Ages History by Yi Pyŏngdo; vol. 3, Modern History by Yi Sangbaek; vol. 4, Contemporary History by Yi Sŏngŭn; vol. 5, Chronological Table, ed. by Chindan Hakhoe; 1959-1962.

Kim Sŏk'yŏng & Others; *Chosŏnsa Kaeyo* (An Outline of Korean History, Kim Ilsŏng University), P'yŏngyang, 1957.

Chosŏn T'ongsa (General History of Korea), ed. by Research Institute of History, Academy of Sciences, P'yŏngyang. vol. 1, 1956 (rev. & enl. ed., 1962); vol. 2, 1958.

Yi Pyŏngdo; *Kuksa Taegwan* (General Outline of Korean History), Seoul, 1958.

Yi Hongjik, Sin Sŏkho, Han Ugŭn & Cho Chwaho; *Kuksa Sin'gang* (New Lectures on Korean History), Seoul, 1958.

Yi Hongjik; *Kuksa Taesajon* (Dictionary of National History), Seoul, 1962. 2 vols.

Kwŏn Sangno; *Han'guk Chimyŏng Yŏnhyŏk-ko* (A Historical Study of Place Names in Korea), Seoul, 1961.

Son Chint'ae; *Han'guk Minjok Sŏrhwaŭi Yŏn'gu* (Studies in the Folklore of Korea), Seoul, 1948. Korean Cultural Series No. 1.

Kim Tuhŏn; *Chosŏn Kajok Chedo Yŏn'gu* (Studies in the Korean Family System), Seoul, 1949. Korean Cultural Series No. 12.

Pak Sihyong; *Chosŏn T'oji Chedo-sa* (History of Korean Land System), P'yŏngyang, 1960-61. 2 vols.

Yi Inyŏng; *Han'guk Manju Kwangyesaŭi Yŏn'gu* (Studies in the History of Korean-Manchurian Relations), Seoul, 1954. Korean Cultural Series No. 13.

Kim Tŭkhwang; *Han'guk Sasangsa* (The History of Thought in Korea), Seoul, 1958.

Chŏng Chinsŏk, Chŏng Sŏngch'ol & Kim Ch'angwŏn;

Chosŏn Ch'olhaksa (A History of Philosophy in Korea), P'yŏngyang, 1960.

Yi Nunhwa; *Han'guk Togyo-sa* (History of Korean Taoism), Seoul, 1960.

Hong Yisŏp, *Chosŏn Kwahaksa* (A History of Korean Science), Seoul, 1946.

Kim Yŏnggi, *Chosŏn Misulsa* (A History of Korean Art), Seoul, 1948.

b) **Ancient Korea**

An Chaehong; *Chosŏn Sanggosagam* (Ancient Korean History), Seoul, 1947-48. 2 vols.

Yi Hongjik; *Han'guk Komunhwa Non'go* (Studies in the Ancient Culture of Korea), Seoul, 1954.

To Yuho; *Chosŏn Wŏnsi Kogohak* (Prehistoric Archaeology in Korea), P'yŏngyang, 1960.

Yujŏk Palgul Pogo (Reports on Excavations of Ancient Sites), Research Institute of Archaeology and Ethnography, Academy of Sciences, P'yŏngyang, 1957-59, 6 vols. seq.

Pak Kyŏngwŏn; *Kyŏngnamŭi Kojŏkkwa Kŭ Munhwa* (On the Historic Remains and Culture of South Kyŏngsang Province), 1955.

Kim Chewon & Youn Moo-Byong; *Uisong Tapni Hobun* (The Ancient Tombs in Tapni Uisong Kun, Kyongsang-pukdo), Seoul, 1962. Special Report of the National Museum of Korea. Vol. 3.

Kim Wŏnyong; *Han'guk Kohwalcha Kaeyo* (Early Movable Type in Korea), Seoul, 1954. Publication of the National Museum of Korea, Series A, No. 1.

Ko Yusŏp; *Han'guk Tapp'aŭi Yŏn'gu* (A Study of Korean Stupas), Seoul, 1948. Korean Cultural Series No. 3.

Yi Yŏsŏng; *Chosŏn Poksikko* (Studies of Korean Clothes), Seoul, 1947.

c) *Three Kingdoms & Unified Silla*

Research Institute of History, Academy of Korea (ed.);
Samguk Sigiŭi Sahoe Kyŏngje Kosŏng-e Kwanhan T'oron-jip (Collected Essays on Socio-Economic Structure in the Three Kingdoms Period), P'yŏngyang, 1958.

Yi Sŏngŭn; *Hwarangdo Yŏn'gu* (Studies of the Whar-hangdo), Seoul, 1949.

National Museum of Korea (ed.); *Kyŏngju Nosŏri Sang-sangch'ong, Mach'ong, 138 hobun Palgul Pogo* (A Report on the Excavation of the Ssangsang Tomb and Tome No. 138), Seoul, 1955.

Kim Wŏnyong; *Studies on Silla Pottery*, Seoul, 1960. Publication of the National Museum of Korea, Series A, No. 4.

Kim Chaewŏn; *Houch'onggwa Ŭllyŏngch'ong* (The Ho-u Tomb and Silver Bell Tomb), Seoul, 1948.

Kim Chewŏn & Youn Moo-Byong; *Kan Eunsa* (A Temple Site of the Silla Dynasty), Seoul, 1961. Report of the National Museum of Korea, No. 2.

Cho Myung-ki; *Silla Pulgyoŭi Inyŏmgua Sasang* (Buddhist Ideology and Thought in Silla), Seoul, 1962.

d) *Koryŏ*

Yi Pyŏngdo; *Koryŏ Sidaeŭi Yŏn'gu* (Studies of the Koryŏ Dynasty), Seoul, 1948. Korean Cultural Series No. 4.

Kim Sanggi; *Tongbang Munhwa Koryousa Non'go* (Studies in the History of Culutral Relations among Asian Countries), Seoul, 1954. Korean Cultural Series No. 8.

Kim Sŏk'yŏng; *Farmers' Struggles against Feudal Controlling Class under the Koryŏ Period*, (in Korean), P'yŏngyang, 1960.

Ko Yusŏp; *Koryŏ Ch'ŏngja* (Koryŏ Celadon), Seoul, 1954.

e) Yi Dynasty

Yi Sangbaek; *Yijo Kŏngugŭi Yŏn'gu* (Studies in the Founding of the Yi Dynasty), Seoul, 1949. Korean Cultural Series No. 9.

Chosŏn Kwahakcha Tongmaeng (ed.); *Yijo Sahoe Kyŏngje-sa* (A Socio-Economic History of the Yi Dynasty), Seoul, 1946.

Ch'oe Hojin; *Kŭndae Choson Kyŏngje-sa Yŏn'gu* (Researches in Recent Korean Economic History), Seoul, 1947.

Cho Ki-zun; *Han'guk Kyŏngje-sa* (History of Korean Economics), Seoul, 1962.

Kim Sŏk'yŏng; *Chosŏn Ponggŏn Sidae Nongminŭi Kyegŭp Kusong* (Class Structure of the Korean Peasants in the Feudal Age), P'yŏngyang, 1957.

Yi Kwangnin; *Yijo Surisa* (History of Irrigation in the Yi Dynasty), Seoul, 1961. Korean Studies Series 8.

Hong Yisŏp; *The Politico-Economic Thought of Yakyong Chŏng, 1762-1836,* (in Korean), Seoul, 1961. Korean Studies Series 3.

Research Institute of History, Academy of Sciences (ed.); *Collected Essays on Chŏng Yakyong,* (in Korean), P'yŏngyang, 1962.

Chŏn Sŏktam & Ch'oe Kugyu; 19 *Segi Hubangi Chosŏn Sahoe Kyŏngjesa* (A History of Korean Society and Economy in the Latter half of the Nineteenth Century), P'yŏngyang, 1959.

Kim Sanggi; *Tonghakkwa Tonghangnan* (Tonghak and the Tonghak Rebellion), Seoul, 1947.

Kim Yŏnggŏn; *Chosŏn Kaehwa Pidam* (Hidden Stories of the Enlightenment of Korea), Seoul, 1947.

Yu Hongryŏl; *Kojong Ch'ihaŭi Sohak Sunanŭi Yŏn'gu* (A Study of Sufferings of Western Learning in King Kojong's Reign), Seoul, 1962.

Hyŏn Sangyun; *Chosŏn Yuhaksa* (History of Korean

Confucianism), Seoul, 1949.

Kim Kyŏngt'ak. *Yulgokŭi Yŏn'gu* (A Study of Yulgok),
Seoul, 1960. Korean Studies Series 7.

[Materials]

Research Institute of Korean Classics, Academy of Korea (ed.); *Classified Excerpts from the Yi Dynasty
Annals (1), Policies 1*, P'yŏngyang, 1960.

Compilation Committee for National History (ed.);
Yi Dynasty Annals, Seoul, 1955-59, 48 vols.

Pibyŏnsa-tŭngrok (The Records of the Office of Military Affairs), Seoul, 1959-60, 28 vols.

Sŭngjŏngwŏn Ilgi (The Dairy of the Royal Secretari-
at), 1961-62 (Vol. 28), seq.

f) *Modern Korea*

Chosŏn Kwahakcha Tongmaeng (ed.); *Chosŏn Haebang-
sa, Samil Undong-p'yŏn* (A History of the Liberation
of Korea; the March 1, 1919 Movement), 1946.

Yi Kŭnjik; *Samil Undongsa* (A History of the March
First Independence Movement), 1955.

Pak Unsik; *Han'guk Tongnip Undong Hyŏlsa* (A History of the Korean Independence Movement), 1946.

Research Institute of History, Academy of Sciences
(ed.); *History of the Just Fatherland Liberation War
of the Korean People*, P'yŏngyang, 1961.

Academy of Sciences (ed.); *Chosŏn Kŭndae Hyŏkmyŏng
Undong-sa* (A History of Revolutional Movements in
Modern Korea), P'yŏngyang, 1961.

2. Western Publications

Hulbert, Homer B.; *The History of Korea*, 1905. New
Edition with an Introduction, Notes and Bibliography
by C. N. Weems, London, 1962. 2 vols.

Griffis, William E.; *Korea, the Hermit Nation*, New
York, 1911. (9th ed. rev. & enl.)

Gale, James S.; *A History of the Korean People*, Seoul, 1927.

McCune, G. M. & Arthur L. Grey, Jr.; *Korea Today*, Harvard University Press, 1950.

Dallet, Charles; *Histoire de l'Eglise de Corée*, Paris, 1874. 2 vols.

Mutel, Gustave; *Documents relatifs aux martyrs de Corée de 1839 et 1846*, Hong Kong, 1924.

Paik, L. George; *The History of Protestant Missions in Korea (1832-1910)*, P'yŏngyang, 1929.

Eckhardt, Andreas; *Geschichte der Koreanischen Kunst*, Leipzig, 1929.

Honey, W. B.; *Korean Pottery*, London, 1947.

3. Japanese Studies in Korean History*

The first of the Japanese works on Korean history of scholarly merit are Hayashi Taisuke's *Chōsen-shi* (History of Korea) published in 1892 and Yoshida Tōgo's *Nikkan Koshi-dan* (Fragments of Old Japanese-Korean History) of the following year. Hayashi's work describes earlier periods up to the fall of the Koryŏ Dynasty. The Yi Dynasty is covered by his later book, *Chōsen Kinsei-shi* (Modern History of Korea). Still later, he put together the two and published a one-volume *Chōsen Tsūshi* (General History of Korea), which, being the very first handbook of Korean history in Japan, was to influence Japanese historians to a great extent.[1] Yoshida's work grasped both Korea and Japan as within a common cultural sphere, a viewpoint that portended, for good or bad, the course later Japanese students of Korean history were to follow.[2]

---

* Adaption of *Le Japon au XIᵉ Congrès International des Sciences Historiques à Stockholm — L'état actuel et les tendances des études historiques au Japon*, Part Two, Chap. II — 1. Korean History, Tokyo, 1960.

After the Russo-Japanese War (1904-05), lectures on Korean history were opened both at the Imperial Universities of Tokyo and Kyoto, precipitating a rapid growth of Japanese scholarship in the field. In Tokyo, Shidehara Taira taught history of Yi Dynasty in 1906, making himself the first Japanese professor ever to give a regular lecture on such topic.[3] His successor Shiratori Kurakichi began to teach early history of Manchuria and Korea in 1912, who was in turn succeeded by Ikeuchi Hiroshi in 1914.[4] In Kyoto, Naitō Torajirō started his lectures on Korean history in 1909, and Imanishi Ryū began to teach ancient history of Korea in 1913.[5] Thus stimuli of big political events such as the Russo-Japanese War and the annexation of Korea (1910) helped the study of Korean history gain a standing as a branch of the studies of broader Asian history by Japanese. In Tokyo the scope of the study included from the beginning Manchuria as well as Korea, with emphasis upon historical geography, and this acted as a framework for years to come. Also approximately at the same time, the Research Department of the South Manchurian Railway Company started scholarly activities under Shiratori's guidance,[6] and field surveys in Korea by Japanese authority became possible. Thus there emerged two groups in the study of Korea: academic works at universities in Japan and on-the-spot researches in Korea and Manchuria.

1920's saw the birth and growth of still another element: In 1924 two seminars on Korean history led by Imanishi Ryū and Oda Shōgo[7] at the new Imperial University of Keijō (Seoul). In 1925 the Government-General of Chōsen expanded its research activities and founded the Chōsen-shi Henshū-kai (Compilation Society for the History of Korea). The two bodies worked hand in hand and built true scholarship in Korea. The most significant of their works are discussed below:

The project of the study of Korean history in the Imperial

University of Keijō included: (a) the reprinting of Korean classics, (b) the publication of studies of the scholars concerned and (c) the investigation of the Yi Dynasty Annals of Korea. Most of the professors participated in the work of the Government-General of Chōsen's Compilation Society for the History of Korea and in the research programme of the Central Council.

The Compilation Society for the History of Korea commenced work in 1924, and in 1932, began publishing the *Chōsen-shi* (Korean History) which was completed in 37 volumes (25,000 pages) in 1940. Since the period covered by *Chōsen-shi* ended on June 27th, 1894, the Society drew up plans, for compiling the history of the sixteen years from that date to the Annexation of Korea on August 22, 1910, not in chronological order but in essay form. The plan was put in execution, but the war ended before it was finished, and its only results were the publication of two research thesis.[8]

The Compilation Society for the History of Korea published, in addition to *Chōsen-shi*, representative selections of the basic historical sources and twenty-one selections were published by 1944.[9]

The research work of the Central Council of the Government-General obtained results in the following four fields: (a) the publication of the geographical texts of the period of the Yi Dynasty and the compilation of their indexes,[10] (b) the textual criticism and publication of the legal books of the period of the Yi Dynasty,[11] (c) the publication of studies of customs and manners,[12] and (d) the completion of the Korean biographical dictionary and its index.[13]

Besides the publications of the Compilation Society and the Central Council, there was *Chōsen-shiryō* (Research Materials) completed by an institue under the direct control of the Government-General of Chōsen. The first number of *Chōsen-shiryō* was published in 1919; the last issue was

No. 47, in 1944.[14]

The sole Japanese institution among the civilian organizations for the study of Korean history was the Seikyū Society, which was founded in 1930. *The Seikyū Gakusō*, its quarterly organ, was issued until October, 1939. A total of about two hundred articles appeared in this journal.

All these organizations were closed at the end of the Pacific War, and, needless to say, Japanese work on Korean history had to undergo great change after this event.

Since the end of the war, the centre of Korean historical studies has been the Toyo Bunko (The Oriental Library). This is partly because the Library possesses a relatively large number of books on Korea, and partly because the Library puts greater emphasis on the study of Korean history than any other organization. Among the postwar publications of the Library there are Maema Kyōsaku's *Kosensappu* (Catalogue of Old Korean Books, a bibliographical study), 3 volumes[15], and Suematsu Yasukazu's *Shinra-shi no Shomondai* (Studies in the History of Silla)[16]. The former is an exhaustive bibliographical study of Korean books, containing more than 2,000 pages. The Library also has carried out the microfilming of Korean books and manuscripts preserved in various libraries in Japan since 1959.

The Gakushūin Tōyōbunka Kenkyūjo (The Gakushuin Institute of Oriental Culture) may be cited as another centre of Korean historical studies. This Institue, which was inaugurated in 1952, aimed as the first stage of its programme at the collection and study of the materials for Korean history; and began publishing in 1953 the popular edition of the Yi Dynasty Annals of Korea. The thirty-six volumes already published covers the period until the end of the reign of King Kojong. This publication will certainly promote rapid progress in the study of Korean history since the fifteen century. The Institute also published the reproduction of *Koryŏ-sa Chŏryo* (Summary of the History of Koryŏ) in

1960.

It should also be mentioned that The Chōsen Gakkai (The Academic Association of Koreanology in Japan) was organized as a public organization for academic research not only on Korean history but also on the problems of Korea today. This Association was founded in October, 1950, with Tenri University in Nara Prefecture as its centre. The association holds annual meetings for the reading of papers and publishes *The Chōsen Gakuhō* (The Journal of the Academic Association of Koreanology) as its quarterly organ.

The Rekishigaku Kenkyūkai (The Historical Science Society) is the third organization interested in Korean history. Testimony as to its interest was given by the issue of *Chōsen-shi no Shomondai* (Problems of Korean History), as a special number of *The Rekishigaku Kenkyū* (The Journal of Historical Studies), its monthly organ, in July, 1953. It is worth mentioning that the Association of Korean Studies, headed by Dr. Mishina Shōei, began to publish *Chōsen Kenkyū Nenpō* (Annual Report of Korean Studies) since 1959, which is characterized for the digested translation of the works by Korean scholars. In addition, the Nihon Chōsen Kenkyūjo (Japanese Institute for Korean Studies) was established in Tokyo in 1961. It intends to promote the study of modern and contemporary Korea.

General survey of the major works on Korean history during and after the War (1937-1962).

General works. Hatada Takashi's *Chōsen-shi* (A History of Korea) presents some critical comments on historical developments after 1910, and one third of the whole book is devoted to the last two chapters, "Korea under the Japanese Rule" and "The Liberation and Agony of the Korean People". It is unique, not only in the fullness and frankness of its treatments of this period, but also in the fullness of its treatment of the social history of Korea[17].

Among the introductory works, there are two books concerning Ancient Korea by Umehara Sueji.[18] Both of them, published immediately after the war, successfully embody the results of thirty years' work in archaeological investigations and excavations by Japanese scholars. Umehara, in cooperation with Fujita Ryōsaku, had been devoting himself since the prewar years to the compilation of *Chōsen Kobunka Sōkan* (General Survey of Korean Antiquities) as the revised edition of the famous *Chōsen Koseki Zufu* (Album of Korean Antiquities).[19] The first three volumes were published after the war.

Prehistoric period. Mikami Tsugio made an inquiry into ancient society and the disposition of the races, comparing the archaeological survey with literary evidence.[20] The conclusion is not complete enough to be persuasive for every reader.[21] Mikami also wrote a monograph on the stone circle in Manchuria and Korea.[22] As for the Korean stone sword and pottery, Arimitsu Kyōichi published the results of his research.[23] There are two opposing views of the well-known problem as to the position of the Chinese province, Chên-fan. Ikeuchi Hiroshi places it in present-day Ch'ungch'ŏng-namdo and Chŏlla-pukto,[24] while Suematsu locates it in Chŏllanamdo and -pukto.[25]

Koguryŏ history. With the activities of Japanese people in Manchuria increasing in and atfer 1931, the history of Koguryŏ was taken up as the major subject of ancient Manchurian history and the ruins in the Chi-an district, its ancient capital, were excavated. One of many reports on it is *Tsūkō* (Tung-kou)[26] coedited by Ikeuchi and Umehara. Ikeuchi wrote thirteen important studies of the history of Koguryŏ,[27] and after the war Mishina also wrote the noteworthy works.[28]

Paekche history. A study of the origins of Paekche by Shiratori Kurakichi whose lectures attracted the attention of the academic world in 1934 was published as a posthumous paper.[29] It elucidates the migration to the south of the Puyo tribe which participated in the founding of Paekche. Ikeuchi's *Nihon Jōdaishi no Ichi Kenkyū* (Studies in the Ancient History of Japan)[30] and Suematsu's *Mimana Kōbōshi* (History of the Rise and Fall of Mimana)[31] inquired into the history of Paekche in relation to Japan. The latter treats the relationship between ancient Korea and Japan with special refernce to Mimana.

Silla history. Mishina's *Shinra Karō no Kenkyū* (Study of Hwarang of Silla)[32] is the first exhaustive study of Silla. Suematsu's *Shinrashi no Shomondai* (Problems of the History of Silla) is a collection of nine treatises and five short articles on the bronze-inscriptions discovered or rediscovered after 1929. Concerning new materials, we must mention first of all the discovery in October, 1933 of the documents on the Silla civil administration kept at the Shōsōin of the Tōdaiji Temple in Nara. An introduction by Nomura Tadao,[33] inspired researchers both at home and abroad.

Koryŏ Dynasty. Suematsu traced the formation of "Yangban" (the nobility), the ruling class of Koryŏ,[34] and made suggestions concerning the rise of the warriors, considering particularly the defence of the northern frontier.[35] Hatada examined the system by which the land was inherited by the eldest legitimate son, while slaves were inherited equally by both sons and daughters,[36] Hanamura Miki attempted to restore the Koryŏ laws to their original form.[37] Aoyama Kōryō and Suematsu clarified the relationships of Koryŏ and Japan,[38] and of Koryŏ and Ming (China).[39]

Early Yi Dynasty (till the sixteenth century). Suematsu corroborated the establishment of the cabinet system (Uichong-pu) in the central political organization,[40] and Naitō Kichinosuke examined the establishment of the legal order in the society under the Yi Dynasty.[41] Fukaya Toshikane studied the character of the landholding system under the Yi Dynasty, and explained the emigration of people to the north-eastern border area in the first half of the fifteenth century.[42] The studies on the tributes and taxation system are the subject of Tagawa Kōzō.[43] Tanaka Takeo probed into the trade relations with Japan in the fifteenth and the sixteenth centuries.[44] Nakamura Hidetaka threw light on the Japanese riots in 1510.[45]

Mid Yi Dynasty (the sixteenth and seventeenth centuries). Shikata Hiroshi analyzed in detail the family register of those days, and elucidated the population, social status, and the cities in comparison with the farming villages.[46] These statistic studies are indeed unique achievements.

Later Yi Dynasty (the nineteenth century). Tabohashi Kiyoshi wrote a voluminous book entitled *Kindai Nissen Kankei-shi* (A History of Japanese-Korean Relations in the Modern Age), and made other studies on the political reform of 1894.[47] Okudaira Takehiko studied the treaty-ports and the Japanese residences,[48] probably as a sequel to his earlier work, *Chōsen Kaikoku Kōshō Shimatsu* (On the Negotiations on the Opening of Korea). Yamaguchi Masayuki made a comprehensive study of the Hwong Sa-yong Letters, the most famous historical materials on Catholicism in Korea.[49]

The Japanese Rule over Korea. Tabohashi discussed the history of the early Japanese rule over Korea,[50] and Matsuoka Shūtarō wrote on the administrative system of the Residency-General,[51] Oda Tadao studied on the financial development of the Government-General of Chōsen,[52] Shizuta Hitoshi treated the development of the banking associations,[53] and Ōuchi Takeji studied rice production.[54] Yamabe Kentarō wrote on the Japanese imperialistic invasion into Korea and the anti-Japanese struggle of the Korean people.[55]

Contemporary Korea. Kawasaki Ichirō discussed the independence of Korea in reference to the Moscow Treaty and the United Nations,[56] and Kamiya Fuji commenced the study on the Korean War.[57]

What must be cited lastly is *Shiryō Shūsei, Tōyōhen* (A

Collection of Historical Documents: Asia), of which the part "Korea" has accounts of historical material and studies of the following items: (a) general works, (b) the period before Three Kingdoms, (c) Three Kingdoms, (d) Koryǒ, (e) the Modern Age, (f) the Period of Japnaese Rule and (g) Korea after the Liberation.[58] This will serve students as both a work of scholarship and an introduction to the study of Korean history.

NOTES

1) Hayashi Taisuke; *Chōsen-shi* (History of Korea), 5 vols., Tokyo, 1892.

ditto; *Chōsen Kindai-shi* (Modern History of Korea), Tokyo, 1901.

ditto; *Chōsen Tsūshi* (General History of Korea), Tokyo, 1912.

2) Yoshida Tōgo; *Nikkan Koshi-dan* (Fragments of Old Japanese-Korean History), Tokyo, 1893.

3) Shidehara Taira; *Kankoku Seisō-shi* (History of Factional Strifes in Korea), Tokyo, 1907.

ditto; *Chōsen Yawa* (Essays on Korean History), Tokyo, 1924.

4) Ikeuchi's numerous articles on history and historical geography of Manchuria and Korea have been published collectively in the following four volumes:

Ikeuchi Hiroshi; *Mansenshi Kenkyū, Jōseihen* (Studies on the History of Manchuria and Korea; Ancient Times), 2 vols., Kyoto (1951), Tokyo (1960).

ditto; *Mansenshi Kenkyū, Chūseihen* (Studies on the History of Manchuria and Korea; Middle Ages), 2 vols., Tokyo, 1943, 37.

5) A number of his works have been posthumously published in the following volumes:

Imanishi Ryū; *Chōsen Koshi no Kenkyū* (Studies in Ancient Korean History), Keijō (Seoul), 1937.

ditto; *Shinra-shi Kenkyū* (Study of the History of Silla), Keijō, 1933.

ditto; *Kudara-shi Kenkyū* (Study of the History of Paekche), Keijō, 1934.

ditto; *Kōrai-shi Kenkyū* (Studies in the History of Koryŏ), Keijō, 1944.

ditto; *Chōsen-shi no Shiori* (A Guide to Korean History), Keijō, 1935.

6) *Man-Sen Chiri Rekishi Kenkyū Hōkoku* (Reports of Studies on Geography and History in Manchuria and Korea), 16 vols., 1915-1941, pub. by the Imperial University of Tokyo.

Tsuda Saukichi; *Chōsen Rekishi-Chiri* (Korean Historical Geography), Tokyo, 1913. 2 vols.

7) Oda Shōgo; *Chōsen Shōshi* (A Short History of Korea), Tokyo, 1931.

8) *Chōsen Tōchishi Ronkō* (Historical Studies on the Japanese Administration in Korea), Keijō, Govt.-Gen. of Chōsen, 1944.

Chōsen Kindaishi Kenkyū (Studies in the History of Modern Korea: Compilation Society for the History of Korea, Monograph Series 1), Keijō, 1944.

9) *Chōsen Shiryō Sōkan* (Korean Historical Materials Series), Keijō, Govt.-Gen. of Chōsen, 1932-1942. 21 vols.

10) *Shinzō Tōgoku Yochi Shōran Sakuin* (Index to the Revised Survey of Korean Geography), Keijō, 1937-1936. 2 vols.

Seisō Jitsuroku Chirishi oyobi Sakuin (Geographical Notes in the Sejong Annals with an Index), Keijō, 1937.

Seizoku Keishōdō Chirishi oyobi Sakuin (Geographical Notes of Kyŏngsangdo and its continued volume with

an Index), Keijō, 1937.
11) *Manki-yoran;* Part I. Finance, 1937; Part II. Military
Administration, 1938; *Jugwanji,* 1939; *Chugyo Taejŏn Hoet'ong* (Annotated Collection of Fundamental
Statutes), 1939; *Sukyo-jupyo,* 1943; *Chōsen Denseikō*
(Studies on the Land System in Korea), 1940; *Ritō-
shūsei* (Collection of Idu), 1937; *Chōsen Saishi
Sōzokuhōron Josetsu* (Studies on Law with Regard
to Inheritance and Religious Observances in Korea;
Introduction), 1939.
12) *Chōsen Fūzoku Shiryō Shūsetsu* (A Collection of Materials on Korean Customs), Keijō, 1937.
Imamura Tomo; *Ri-chō Jitsuroku Fūzoku Kankei Shiryō Saiyō* (Selection of Materials Related to Customs in the Yi Dynasty Annals), Keijō, 1944.
Kōrai Izen no Fūzoku Kankei Shiryō Saiyō (Selection
of Materials Related to Customs before the Koryŏ
Dynasty), Keijō, 1946.
13) *Chōsen Jinmei Jisho* (Korean Biographical Dictionary),
Keijō, 1937; *Index,* Keijō, 1939.
14) *e.g.* No. 44, Village Festivals, 1937; No. 45, Sacrifices
to Confucius; Prayers for Rain; Sacrifices to Family
Spirits, 1938; No. 47, Rural Amusement in Korea,
1944.
15) Maema Kyōsaku; *Kosen Sappu* (Catalogue of Old Korean Books, a bibliographical study) Tokyo, The
Toyo Bunko, Vol. I (1944); Vol. 2 (1956); Vol. 3
(1957). A word should be added about the highly
meritorious achievements by Maema Kyōsaku, who,
without any help from academic instituitons, studied
Korean language and raised an impressive collection
of Korean books while living in Korea for many
years.
16) Suematsu Yasukazu; *Shinra-shi no Shomondai* (Studies in the History of Silla), Tokyo, The Toyo Bunko,

1954.

17) Hatada Takashi; *Chōsen-shi* (A History of Korea), Tokyo, 1951.

18) Umehara Sueji; *Chōsen Kodai no Bunka* (Ancient Culture in Korea), Kyoto, 1946.

ditto; *Chōsen Kodai no Bosei* (Funeral Practices in Ancient Korea), Tokyo, 1947.

19) *Chōsen Koseki Zufu* (Album of Korean Antiquities), Keijō, Govt.-Gen. of Chōsen, 1915-1935. 15 vols.

Umehara Sueji & Fujita Ryōsaku; *Chōsen Kobunka Sōkan* (General Survey of Korean Antiquities), Tenri, Vol. 1 (1946); Vol. 2 (1957); Vol. 3 (1959), seq.

Other publications on Korean Archaeology by R. Fujita are:

Fujita Ryōsaku; *Chōsen Kōkogaku Kenkyū* (Studies in Korean Archaeology), Kyoto, 1948.

ditto; *Chōsengaku Ronkō* (Collected Essays on Korean Studies by the late Dr. Fujita), Nara, 1963.

20) Mikami Tsugio; "Kaijin to sono Minzokuteki Seikaku ni tsuite" (Wai-in and its Racial Characters), *Chōsen-gakuhō* 2-3, 1951-52.

ditto; "Chōsen-hantō ni okeru Shisekibo no arikata ni tsuite" (On the Dolmen in the Korean Peninsula), *Shingaku-zasshi* 62-4, 1953.

ditto; "Taikyū no Shisekibogun to Kodai Nansen Shakai" (The Social Structure in Ancient South Korea and the Dolmen Group), *Tōhōgaku-ronshū* 2, 1954.

ditto; "Eishi Chōsenkoku no Seiji Shakaiteki Seikaku (Political and Social Structure of Korea under the Yui Dynasty), in *Chūgoku Kodaishi no Shomondai*, Tokyo, 1954.

21) Mishina Shōei; "Kaihakuzoku Shōkō" (Some Observations on the Wai-Bak Tribes, in Relation with the Critical Study of the Ethnographical Bibliographies), *Chōsen-gakuhō* 4, 1954.

22) Mikami Tsugio; *Mansen Genshi Funbo no Kenkyū* (The Dolmen and Stone Sites in Manchuria and Korea), Tokyo, 1961.

23) Arimitsu Kyōichi; *Chōsen Masei-sekken no Kenkyū* (A Study of the Korean Polished Stone Sword), Kyoto Univ., 1959.

ditto; *Chōsen Kushimemon-doki no Kenkyū* (The Kushimemon Pottery of Korea), Kyoto Univ., 1962.

24) Ikeuchi Hiroshi; "Shinbangun no Ichi ni tsuite" (On the Location of Chen-fan Province), *Shigaku-zasshi* 57-2, 3, 1948.

25) Suematsu Yasukazu; "Kan Shinbangun Chi Kō" (An Attempts at Presuming the Location of the Chen-fan District under the Han Dynasties), *Kodaigaku* 1-3, 1952.

26) Ikeuchi Hiroshi; *Tsūkō* (Tung-kou, Ancient Koguryŏ Site in Chi-an District), Vol. 1, Tokyo, 1938; Ikeuchi Hiroshi & Umehara Suiji; *Tsūkō* (Tung-kou), Vol. 2, 1940.

As for the prewar Japanese studies on Korean archaeology, refer the following two series of reports:

Koseki Chōsa Hōkoku (Reports of Investigation of Ancient Remains), Keijō, Govt.-Gen. of Chōsen, 1917-1940. 16 vols.

Koseki Chōsa Tokubetsu Hōkoku (Special Report of Investigation of Ancient Remains), Keijō, Govt.-Gen. of Chōsen, 1919-1929, 6 vols.

Koseki Chōsa Tokubetsu Hōkoku (Special Report of Investigation of Ancient Remains), Keijō, Govt.-Gen. of Chōsen, 1919-1929, 6 vols.

27) See Ikeuchi's *Mansenshi Kenkyū Jōseihen*, mentioned-above in (4).

28) Mishina Shōei; "Kōkuri Ōto Kō" (Observations on the Capital of the Koguryŏ Dynasty), *Chōsen-gakuhō* 1, 1951.

ditto; "Sangokushiki Kōkuri Hongi no Gentenhihan" (Text-critique of the Koguryŏ Annals in the Samkuk-saki), *Ōtanidaigaku-kenkyū-nenpō* 6, 1954.

29) Shiratori Kurakichi; "Kudara no Kigen ni tsuite" (On the Origins of Paekche), *Shigaku* 1, 1947.

30) Ikeuchi Hiroshi; *Nihon Jōdaishi no Ichi Kenkyū* (Studies in the Ancient History of Japan), Tokyo, 1947.

31) Suematsu Yasukazu; *Mimana Kōbōshi* (History of the Rise and Fall of Mimana), Tokyo, 1956, rev. ed.

32) Mishina Shōei; *Chōsen Kodai Kenkyū Daiichibu, Shinra Karō no Kenkyū* (Studies of Ancient Korea, Part One; Study of Hwarang of Silla), Tokyo, 1943.

33) Nomura Tadao; "Shōsōin yori Hakken sareta Shiragi no Minseimonjo ni tsuite" (The Administrative Documents of Silla discovered at Shōsōin), *Shigaku-zassi* 62-4, 1953.

34) Suematsu Yasukazu; "Kōrai shoki no Ryōhan ni tsuite" (On Yangban, or the Nobility at the Early Period of the Koryŏ Dynasty), *Tōyō-gakuhō*, 36-2, 1953.

35) ditto; "Kōrai Heibashi Kō" (Considerations on the Pyong-ma-sa during the Koryŏ Period), *Tōyō-gakuhō* 39-1, 1956.

36) Hatada Takashi; "Kōrai-jidai ni okeru Tochi no Chakuchōshi Sōzoku to Nuhi no Shijo Kinbun Sōzoku" (The Inheritance Law under the Koryŏ Dynasty), *Tōyōbunka* 22, 1957.

37) Hanamura Miki; "Kōrai Ritsu" (The Law under the Koryŏ Dynasty), in *Chōsen Shakai Hōseishi Kenkyū*, Tokyo, 1937.

38) Aoyama Kōryō, "Nichirai Kōshōshi no Kenkyū" (Studies on the History of Koryŏ-Japanese Intercourse), *Meiji Daigaku Bungakubu Kenkyūhōkoku, Tōyōshi* 3, 1955.

39) Suematsu Yasukazu, "Raimatsu Sensho ni okeru Taimin Kankei" (The Korean Relations with the Ming

Dynasty in the Later Koryŏ and Early Yi Dynasty
Periods), *Shigaku-ronsō* 2, 1941.

40) ditto, "Chōsen Giseifu Kō" (Study of the Cabinet
System under the Yi Dynasty), *Chōsen-gakuhō* 9,
1956.

41) Naitō Kichinosuke; "Keikoku-taiten no Nanzan" (On
the Compilation of Kyŏngkuk-taejon), in: *Chōsen
Shakai Hōseishi*, Tokyo, 1937.

42) Fukaya Toshikane; "Chōsen no Minden ni tsuite" (On
the Landholding System under the Yi Dynasty), in:
Tōyō Nōgyō Keizaishi Kenkyū, Tokyo, 1948.

ditto; "Chōsen Sesōchō ni okeru Tōhoku-henkyō eno
Dai-ichiji Shimin Nyūkyo ni tsuite" (The First
Emigration to the North-eastern Frontier during
Sejong's Reign of the Yi Dynasty), *Chōsengakuhō*
9, 1956.

43) Tagawa Kōzō; "Richō Kōbutsu Kō" (Taxation and
Tribute under the Yi Dynasty), *Chōsen-gakuhō* 9,
1956. A number of his articles are prepared in one
volume entitled *Richō Kōbutsu no Kenkyū* (Studies
in the Taxation and Tributes under the Yi Dynasty),
which will shortly be published by the Toyo Bunko.

44) Tanaka, Takeo; "Shoki Nissen Kōtsū to Hakata Bōeki
Shōnin (The Japanese-Korean Intercourse during
the Early Years of the Yi Dynasty and the Hakata
Merchants), *Chōsen-gakuhō* 4, 1853.

ditto; "Rishi Sesōchō ni okeru Nissen Kōtsū no Shomondai" (The Japanese-Korean Intercourse under
the Sejong's Reign), *Tōhōgaku* 8, 1954.

ditto; "Chūsei Nissen Kōtsū ni okeru Bōekiken no Suii"
(The History of the Trade Rights in the Japanese-
Korean Trade during the Medieval Ages), *Shigaku-
zasshi* 63-3, 1954.

45) Nakamura Hidetaka; "1510-nen Chōsen Sanpo ni okeru
Nihonjin no Sōran" (The Japanese Riot at Sampo,

or Three Ports), *Nagoyadaigaku Bungakubu Kenkyū-ronshū* 2, 1952.

46) Shikata Hiroshi; "Richō Jinkō ni Kansuru Ichikenkyū" (On the Population under the Yi Dynasty), in Chō-*sen Shakai Hōseishi Kenkyū*, Tokyo, 1937.

ditto; "Richō Jinkō ni kansuru Mibun Kaikyū-betsuteki Kansatsu" (The Population under the Yi Dynasty and the Social Classes), in *Chōsen Keizai no Kenkyū* (Studies in Economy of Korea) 3, Tokyo, 1938.

ditto; "Richō-jidai no Toshi to Nōson toni kansuru Ichishiron" (A Study on the City and Rural Villages under the Yi Dynasty), *Keijō-Teikokudaigaku Hō-gakkai-ronshū* 12-3. 4, 1941.

47) Tabohashi Kiyoshi; *Kindai Nissen Kankeishi* (A History of Japanese-Korean Relations in the Modern Age), Keijō, 1940. 2 vols.

ditto; "Kindai Chōsen ni okeru Seijiteki Kaikaku, 1" (Political Reformation in Modern Korea, 1), in *Kindai Chōsenshi Kenkyū* (Studies in the Modern History of Korea), Keijō, 1944.

48) Okudaira Takehiko; "Chōsen no Jōyakukō to Koryū-chi" (The Open Ports and Foreign Settlements in Korea), in *Chōsen Shakai Hōseishi Kenkyū*, Tokyo, 1937.

49) Yamaguchi Masayuki; *Kōshiei Hakusho no Kenkyū* (Studies in the Secret Letters of Hwong Sayong), Kyoto, 1941.

50) Tabohashi Kiyoshi; *Chōsen Tōchishi Ronkō* (Historical Studies in the Administration of Korea), Keijō, 1944.

51) Matsuoka Shūtarō; "Tōkanfu no Tōchihōsei" (The Administration System of the Japanese Residency-General in Korea), *Keijō-Teikokudaigaku Hōgakkai-ronshū* 12-3, 1941.

52) Oda Tadao; "Heigōshoki ni okeru Chōsen Sōtokufu Zaisei no Hattatsu" (The Development in the Finance

of the Government-General of Chōsen during the Early Years of the Japanese Annexation), in *Chōsen Keizai no Kenkyū* 3, Tokyo, 1938.

ditto; "Bunkaseiji-ki ni okeru Chōsen Sōtokufu Zaisei no Hattatsu" (The Development in the Finance of the Government-General of Chōsen in the Reign of Admiral Viscount Saitō), *Keijō-Teikokudaigaku Hōgakkai-ronshū* 14-1, 1943.

53) Shizuta Hitoshi; "Chōsen ni okeru Kin'yū-kumiai no Hattatsu" (The Development of the Banking Union in Korea), in *Chōsenkeizai no Kenkyū* 3, Tokyo, 1938.

54) Ōuchi Takeji; "Chōsen ni okeru Beikoku Seisan" (Rice Production in Korea), in *ibid.*, 1938.

55) Yamabe Kentarō; "Nihon Teikokushugi no Chōsen Shinryaku to Chōsen-jinmin no Hankō Tōsō" (The Japanese Imperialism into Korea and the Resistance Movement of Korean People), *Rekishigaku-kenkyū—Chōsenshi no Shomondai*, 1953.

ditto; "3.1 Undō ni tsuite" (On the March First Movement), *Rekishigaku-kenkyū*, 184, 185, 1955.

ditto; "3.1 Undō to sono Gendaiteki Igi" (The March First Movement and its Historical Meaning), *Shisō* 372, 373, 1955.

56) Kawasaki Ichirō; "Mosukuwa Kyōtei to Chōsen Dokuritsu" (The Moscow Agreement and the Independence of Korea), *Kokusai-seiji-jihō* 20, 1956.

ditto; "Kokusai-rengō to Chōsen Dokuritsu" (The Independence of Korea and the United Nations), *Kokusaiseiji-jihō* 21, 1956.

57) Kamiya Fuji; "Chōsen-sensō Zenshi" (A Political History Prior to the Korean War), *Hōgaku-zasshi* 4-1, 1957.

58) *Shiryō-shūsei, Tōyōshi-hen* (A Collection of Historical Documents, Volume of Asian History), Tokyo, Heibonsha, 1955.

APPENDIX II

CHRONOLOGICAL LIST OF RULERS
OF KOREAN DYNASTIES

A. *Koguryŏ* (? 37 B.C.–668 A.D.)

1. Tongmyŏngsŏng Wang
   (37 B.C.–19 B.C.)
2. Yurimyŏng Wang
   (19 B.C.–18 A.D.)
3. Taemusin Wang (18– 44)
4. Minjung Wang (44– 48)
5. Mobon Wang (48– 53)
6. T'aejo Wang (53–146)
7. Ch'adae Wang (146–165)
8. Sindae Wang (165–179)
9. Kogukch'ŏn Wang (179–197)
10. Sangsang Wang (197–227)
11. Tongch'ŏn Wang (227–248)
12. Chungch'ŏn Wang (248–270)
13. Soch'ŏn Wang (270–292)
14. Pongsang Wang (292–300)

15. Mich'ŏn Wang (300–331)
16. Kogugwŏn Wang (331–371)
17. Sosurim Wang (371–384)
18. Kogugyang Wang (384–391)
19. Kwanggaet'o Wang
   (391–412)
20. Changsu Wang (413–491)
21. Munja Wang (492–519)
22. Anjang Wang (519–531)
23. Anwŏn Wang (531–545)
24. Yang-wŏn Wang (545–559)
25. P'yŏng-wŏn Wang (559–590)
26. Yŏng-yang Wang (590–618)
27. Yŏngnyu Wang (618–642)
28. Pojang Wang (642–668)

B. *Paekche* (? 18 B.C.–660 A.D.)

1. Onjo Wang
   (18 B.C.–28 A.D.)
2. Taru Wang (28– 77)
3. Kiru Wang (77–128)
4. Kaeru Wang (128–166)
5. Ch'ogo Wang (166–214)
6. Kusu Wang (214–234)
7. Saban Wang (234)
8. Koi Wang (234–286)

9. Chaekkye Wang (286–298)
10. Punsŏ Wang (298–304)
11. Piryu Wang (304–344)
12. Ke Wang (344–346)
13. Kŭnch'ogo Wang (346–375)
14. Kŭn-gusu Wang (375–384)
15. Ch'imnyu Wang (384–385)
16. Chinsa Wang (385–392)
17. Asin Wang (392–405)

18. Chŏnji Wang	(405–420)	26. Sŏng Wang	(523–554)
19. Kuisin Wang	(420–427)	27. Widŏk Wang	(554–598)
20. Piyu Wang	(427–455)	28. Hye Wang	(598–599)
21. Kaero Wang	(455–475)	29. Pŏp Wang	(599–600)
22. Munju Wang	(475–477)	30. Mu Wang	(600–645)
23. Samgŭn Wang	(477–479)	31. Ŭija Wang	(645–660)
24. Tongsŏng Wang	(479–501)	32. P'ungjang Wang	(660–663)
25. Munyŏng Wang	(501–523)		

C. *Silla* (? 57 B.C.–935 A.D.)

1. Hyŏkkŏse Wang		15. Kirim Wang	(298–310)
	(57 B.C.–3 A.D.)	16. Hŭlhae Wang	(310–356)
2. Namhae Wang	(4– 24)	17. Naemul Wang	(356–402)
3. Yuri Wang	(24– 57)	18. Silsŏng Wang	(402–417)
4. T'alhae Wang	(57– 80)	19. Nulchi Wang	(417–458)
5. P'asa Wang	(80–112)	20. Chabi Wang	(458–479)
6. Chima Wang	(112–134)	21. Soji Wang	(479–500)
7. Ilsŏng Wang	(134–154)	22. Chijŭng Wang	(500–514)
8. Adalla Wang	(154–184)	23. Pŏphŭng Wang	(514–540)
9. Pŏrhyu Wang	(184–196)	24. Chinhŭng Wang	(540–576)
10. Naehae Wang	(196–230)	25. Chinji Wang	(576–579)
11. Chobun Wang	(230–247)	26. Chinp'yŏng Wang	(579–632)
12. Ch'ŏmhae Wang	(247–261)	27. Sŏndŏk Yŏwang	(632–647)
13. Mich'u Wang	(262–284)	28. Chindŏk Yowang	(647–654)
14. Yurye Wang	(284–298)	29. Muryŏl Wang	(654–661)

C'. *Unified Silla* (661 A.D.–935 A.D.)

30. Munmu Wang	(661–681)	37. Sŏndŏk Wang	(780–785)
31. Sinmun Wang	(681–692)	38. Wŏnsŏng Wang	(785–798)
32. Hyoso Wang	(692–702)	39. Sosŏng Wang	(799–800)
33. Sŏngdŏk Wang	(702–737)	40. Aejang Wang	(800–809)
34. Hyosŏng Wang	(737–742)	41. Hŏndŏk Wang	(809–826)
35. Kyŏngdŏk Wang	(742–765)	42. Hŭngdŏk Wang	(826–836)
36. Hyesong Wang	(765–780)	43. Hŭigang Wang	(836–838)

44. Minae Wang	(838–839)	51. Chinsŏng Yŏwang	(887–897)
45. Sinmu Wang	(839)	52. Hyogong Wang	(897–912)
46. Munsŏng Wang	(839–857)	53. Sindŏk Wang	(912–917)
47. Hŏnan Wang	(857–861)	54. Kyŏngmyŏng Wang	
48. Kyŏngmun Wang	(861–875)		(917–924)
49. Hŏn-gang Wang	(875–886)	55. Kyŏng-ae Wang	(924–927)
50. Chŏnggang Wang	(886–887)	56. Kyŏngsun Wang	(927–935)

D. *Koryŏ* (918–1392 A.D.)

1. T'aejo (Wang kŏn)		20. Sinjong	(1197–1204)
	(918– 943)	21. Hŭijong	(1204–1211)
2. Hyejong	(943– 945)	22. Kangjong	(1211–1213)
3. Chŏngjong	(945– 949)	23. Kojong	(1213–1259)
4. Kwangjong	(949– 975)	24. Wŏnjong	(1259–1274)
5. Kyŏngjong	(975– 981)	25. Ch'ungnyŏl Wang	
6. Sŏngjong	(981– 997)		(1274–1308)
7. Mokchong	(997–1009)	26. Ch'ungsŏn Wang	(1308–1313)
8. Hyŏnjong	(1009–1031)	27. Ch'ungsuk Wang	(1313–1330)
9. Tŏkjong	(1031–1034)	28. Ch'unghye	((1331–1332)
10. Chŏngjong	(1034–1046)	Wang	((1339–1344)
11. Munjong	(1046–1082)	29. Ch'ungmok Wang	
12. Sunjong	(1082–1083)		(1344–1348)
13. Sŏnjong	(1083–1094)	30. Ch'ungjŏng Wang	
14. Hŏnjong	(1094–1095)		(1348–1351)
15. Sukjong	(1095–1105)	31. Kongmin Wang	(1351–1374)
16. Yejong	(1105–1122)	32. Sin-u	(1374–1388)
17. Injong	(1122–1146)	33. Sinch'ang	(1389)
18. Ŭijong	(1146–1170)	34. Kongyang Wang	(1389–1392)
19. Myŏngjong	(1170–1197)		

E. *Chosŏn* (1392–1910 A.D.)

1. T'aejo (Yi Sŏnggye)		3. T'aejong	(1400–1418)
	(1392–1399)	4. Sejong	(1418–1450)
2. Chŏngjong	(1399–1400)	5. Munjong	(1450–1452)

6.	Tanjong	(1452–1455)	17.	Hyojong	(1649–1659)
7.	Sejo	(1455–1468)	18.	Hyŏnjong	(1659–1674)
8.	Yejong	(1468–1469)	19.	Sukchong	(1674–1720)
9.	Sŏngjong	(1469–1494)	20.	Kyŏngjong	(1720–1724)
10.	Yŏnsan-gun	(1494–1506)	21.	Yŏngjo	(1724–1776)
11.	Chungjong	(1506–1544)	22.	Chŏngjo	(1776–1800)
12.	Injong	(1544–1545)	23.	Sunjo	(1804–1834)
13.	Myŏngjong	(1545–1567)	24.	Hŏnjong	(1834–1849)
14.	Sŏnjo	(1567–1608)	25.	Ch'oljong	(1849–1863)
15.	Kwanghae-gun	(1608–1623)	26.	Kojong	(1864–1907)
16.	Injo	(1623–1649)	27.	Sunjong	(1907–1910)

CHINESE PROVINCES
AND
THE THREE HANS
⊠ Ancient Sites

PUYŎ

LONG
WHITE
MT.

TUMEN RIVER

H·SÜAN·T'U

YALU RIVER

ŎK CHO

TAEDONG RIVER

L
O
(Pyŏngyang)
L
A
N
G
[TAI-FANG]

LIN-TUN

YE

HAN RIVER

MAHAN

CH'ĚN-FAN

KŬM RIVER

CH'ĚN
HAN

NAKTONG RIVER

PIEN
CH'ĚN

(Kimhae)

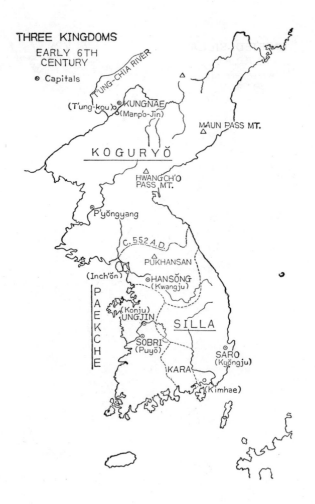

THREE KINGDOMS

EARLY 6TH
CENTURY

◉ Capitals

T'UNG-CHIA RIVER

(T'ung-kou) ◉KUNGNAE
(Manp'o-Jin)

MAUN PASS MT.

K O G U R Y Ŏ

HWANGCH'O
PASS MT.

P'yŏngyang

C. 552 A.D.

PUKHANSAN

(Inch'ŏn) ◉HANSŎNG
(Kwangju)

P
A
E
K
C
H
E

(Konju)
UNGJIN

SILLA

◉SŎBRI
(Puyŏ)

SARO
(Kyŏngju)

KARA

(Kimhae)

UNIFIED SILLA
IN 750 A.D.
⊙ NINE PROVINCIAL
   CAPITALS

PO-HAI

TUMEN RIVER

YALU RIVER

TAEDONG RIVER

HAN RIVER

SAKCHU

MYŎNGJU

PUKWŎN

HANJU

UNGJU

SANGJU

CH'ŎNGJU

SARO
(Kyŏngju)

KANGJU

YANGJU

MUJU

CH'ŎNGHAE
(Wando)

KORYŎ
12TH CENTURY

5 PROVINCES &
2 TERRITORIES

JURCHIN

LONG FORTRESSES

PUKKYE

HAMGYŎNG

CHŎNGP'YŎNG

SŎGYŎNG
(Pyŏngyang)

SŎHAE-DO

TONGGYE

MTS. CHABI

YESONG RIVER

KYOJU
-DO

KAEGYŎNG

KANGHWA

YANGGWANG-DO

KYŎNGSANG
I-DO

MT. KAYA

CHŎLLA-DO

KŬMJU
(Kimhae)

HAPP'O
(Masan)

TSUSHIMA

TAMNA

YI DYNASTY

- Six Fortresses
- ★ Four Provinces
- ○ Three Ports

ONSŎNG
CH'ANGSŎNG
K'YŎNGWŎN
HOENYONG
K'YŎNGHUNG
PUNYŎNG

UYE YŎYŎN
CHASŎNG MUCH'ANG

HAMGYŎNG-DO

P'YŎNGAN-DO

YŎNGHŬNG

P'YŎNGYANG
CH'OLLYŎNG

HWANGHAE-DO △O'TAE-SAN
KANGWŎN-DO
(Seoul)
KANGHWA KYŎNGSŎNG
SAMCHŎNGDO
KWANGJU T'AEPAEK-SAN

CHUNGCH'ŎNG
-DO
KYŎNGSANG
-DO
CHŎKSANG-SAN
YŎMP'O

CHŎLLA
-DO
PUSANP'O
(Pusan)
NAEIP'O TSUSHIMA
(Ungch'on)
NAGOYA
KYŪSHŪ

MODERN KOREA

[CHAKANG-DO]

YANGKANG-DO

HAMGYŎNG -PUKTO

P'YŎNGAN -PUKTO

HAMGYŎNG -NAMDO

P'YŎNGAN NAMDO

⊡P'YŎNGYANG

HWANGHAE

[NAMDO] [PUKTO]

KWANWŎN-DO

38°

SEOUL ⊡

KANGHWA

INCH'ŎN KYŎNGGI -DO

CHUNGCHŎNG -PUKTO

NAMDO KYŎNGSANG -PUKTO

CHŎLLA PUKTO

KYŎNGSANG -NAMDO

CHŎLLA NAMDO

CHEJU-DO